THE DEMON LOVER

73660

THE

DEMON LOVER

A PSYCHOANALYTICAL APPROACH

TO LITERATURE

BY

ARTHUR WORMHOUDT, Ph. D.

INTRODUCTION BY EDMUND BERGLER, M.D.

Essay Index Reprint Series

BOOKS FOR LIBRARIES PRESS
FREEPORT, NEW YORK

INTERNATIONAL STANDARD BOOK NUMBER
0-8369-1011-7

LIBRARY OF CONGRESS CATALOG CARD NUMBER:
68-29256

PRINTED IN THE UNITED STATES OF AMERICA

FOR PEARL

ACKNOWLEDGMENT

I am indebted to the Oxford University Press for permission to quote from the *Letters of John Keats*, edited by Maurice Buxton Forman and to Charles Scribner and Sons for a passage from *Byron*, by Ethel Colburn Mayne. I also wish to express my thanks to Professor Lionel Trilling who read a part of the manuscript. I am particularly indebted to Dr. Edmund Bergler whose theories underlie this book, for his reading of the entire manuscript and the many specific suggestions which he offered.

CONTENTS

FOREWORD

Dr. Wormhoudt has, in *The Demon Lover*, made a systematic attempt to apply some of the newer findings of psychoanalytic psychiatry to the Romantic poets. I have read the book with great interest; it does for its field what practicing psychoanalysts can not do. A physician who is "also" interested in literature does not and can not have the wide knowledge demanded of the specialist in comparative literature. And yet this book is fully in line with Freud's aim for applied psychoanalysis: analyzed specialists in each field applying analysis to their circumscribed orbits. Dr. Wormhoudt's method is a precise realization of that aim. The reader of the book is not asked to believe in every detail or in the general deductions. He is invited to judge for himself how unconscious reactions of poets, as expressed in their poems, which were previously dismissed as meaningless or "oversights" on the part of the poet, acquire a very specific meaning if viewed in the light of modern psychiatry.

EDMUND BERGLER, M.D.

THE DEMON LOVER

But oh! that deep romantic chasm which slanted
Down the green hill athwart a cedarn cover!
A savage place! as holy and enchanted
As e'er beneath a waning moon was haunted
By woman wailing for her demon lover!

KUBLA KHAN

I

INTRODUCTION

THE value of psychoanalysis for the explication of particular works of literature has not as yet been generally accepted among scholars and students. Not that anyone questions the fact that the human mind is divided into conscious and unconscious areas which are distinct from each other. Nor is there disagreement over the fact that literature springs largely from the unconscious department of the mind. Neither of these ideas is exactly new. As far back as Leibnitz and earlier it had been suggested that the mind had other than conscious powers. Plato had spoken of the poet as someone subject to a "divine enthusiasm" and thus pointed to the truth that the poet's lack of conscious control over the sources of his inspiration was really due to the compulsive tendencies which underlie consciousness in the realms of the unconscious. The poets themselves had of course given Plato the clue to this observation. It is not for nothing that Homer calls upon the muse to sing his song of Troy and Odysseus. He knows that his conscious mind can do little more than give form and order to what springs from some other-than-conscious source—the muse. So, too, Shakespeare speaks wittily but truly of "the poet's eye in a fine frenzy rolling." Goethe and Nietzsche add their testimony.[1] One might extend the list of quotations indefinitely.

How does it happen, then, that there has been so little attempt made to discover more precisely the unconscious sources of literature? Why have poets and commentators alike been content merely to note that there is an unconscious source and do little toward exploring it? We may correlate this question with another which may shed some light upon it. Most of the discoveries of modern psychology about the unconscious were made as the result of detailed analyses of subjective reports of individual mental life. This technique brought to light the fact that conscious mental life was continually disturbed by conflicting impulses and motivations which could be understood in terms of unconscious tendencies. Now since literature is one of the most sensitive reproductions of mental life that we have, how does it happen that the detailed study to which it has long been subjected never revealed these basic unconscious tendencies? How does it happen that there is so little detailed explanation of the psychological inconsistencies on the conscious level which close study reveals in many great works of art? For the history of criticism shows very few examples of detailed psychological analyses of actual texts. Critics have usually concerned themselves with value judgments, vague generalities, or purely factual comment. The reason for Hamlet's delay, for example, has always puzzled critics and commentators, and various theories have been adduced to explain it. But no one, before Freud invented the technique of psychoanalysis, seems to have hit upon the solution that Hamlet's unconscious attachment to his mother accounts plausibly for the delay and a good many other puzzling factors in the play.

There are indeed many reasons why the unconscious elements in a work of literature are difficult to isolate and make sense out of; but the most important of them is that the unconscious resistance which prevents the writer from being aware of his own unconscious tendencies also prevents the reader from recognizing them in the finished work of art. This does not mean that these unconscious elements have no effect on the reader. On the contrary, they are indispensable to the total effect of the work. But it is when we cease to appreciate the work in a passive and uncritical manner that we begin to feel the need to understand and consequently the need for some more adequate technique of psychological analysis than that which describes the workings of the conscious mind. Within the last fifty years such a technique has been elaborated and tested by the psychoanalysts, but the results of their researches have not yet been fully applied or even understood by literary scholars. In recent times, therefore, it is not merely unconscious resistances which prevent the understanding of unconscious elements in literature: there have been misunderstandings of psychoanalytical theory and inadequate attempts to apply it to specific works. With regard to the latter it is perhaps enough to say that no analysis of a literary work can be of much use which does not treat the work in a detailed manner. Such minute analysis may sometimes strike the reader as boring and unnecessary, but its value in increased understanding of the work of art itself will also be evident.

Misunderstandings in psychoanalytical theory, however, must first be clarified before the technique can be profitably employed. One of the first phenomena of mental life to which Freud applied his ability to analyze the psyche was the dream. In the course of his investigations it became apparent that dreams and literature have a good deal in common. Both express their meanings via certain symbolic constructions and this implies that their meanings undergo a great deal of displacement and condensation. Both these characteristics are typical of the unconscious source of dreams and literature. Conscious thought tends to denude its symbols of the rich complexity which clings to unconscious symbols, and it seeks to prevent condensation by means of discursive and analytical reasoning. But the real problem with which Freud was confronted in analyzing dreams was how to find a common denominator for the bewildering maze of symbols and tendencies which dreams displayed. As is well known, he first came to the conclusion that dreams are expressions of wish fulfillments. That is to say, Freud found that dreams could be most consistently interpreted if they are understood as attempts to gratify libidinous tendencies which are forbidden by the unconscious censor, which in turn represents society's control over the individual.

The value of this insight into the nature of dreams was very great and Freud was quick to make the application to literature. As we have already noted, he was able to solve the much-vexed problem of why Hamlet delays by laying stress on Hamlet's unconscious libidinous attachment to his mother. This attachment is forbidden by Hamlet's inner conscience and he is consequently torn between the desire to gratify his libidinous wishes which imply the death of his father and stepfather, and his desire to curb them which means failure to avenge his father's death. Since the oedipus pattern is one which is very common in literature, it is easy to see that Freud had made a real discovery in the technique of literary and psychological analysis. The procedure might be formulated in some such terms as the following. First look for the unconscious libidinous wish and its symbolic expression, then discover how the censor has attempted to prohibit the wish.

But this analysis had its limitations. At this point in his researches Freud was chiefly interested in the libidinous tendencies of the unconscious. In his interpretation of Hamlet, for example, it is plain that these are said to be the primary motivating factor. The prohibiting censor was, after all, originally a force external to the psyche and its unconscious power to inhibit and repress libidinous tendencies seemed to come not from the psyche itself but from the constant external pressure of society. At least this was what many people thought Freud was saying and what led to the most common misconception of psychoanalytic technique: that it is a method of tracking down the transformations and symbols of man's sexual instincts.[2] Such a view is plainly an oversimplification as some of Freud's critics still point out. What they do not realize, however, is that Freud and his fellow psychoanalysts went on to discover other components of the psyche which are just as important as the libidinous ones.

Freud's later views on these topics were not formulated until late in life and were not published with full clinical reports as, for example, *The Interpretation of Dreams* was.[3] Nevertheless in his Eros-Thanatos theory he was just as scientifically minded as in his earlier views. According to this theory the psyche is composed of two dominant instincts: the libidinous which includes ego-directed tendencies and object-directed ones, and the aggressive which may also be directed against the self or against others. It will be seen that on the basis of this new theory Freud is no longer laying sole stress on the sexual instincts. Aggression has now taken its place alongside libido as a tendency equally worthy of study. The censor is no longer a mere internalization of external social forces: it now derives its power from just as basic and integral an element of the psyche as the libidinous tendencies—that is, from the thanatic element.

The consequences of this enlargement in the scope of psychoanalytic theory are important for the interpretation of dreams and literature. To take the example of Hamlet again, we can now see that there are certain aspects of the motivation of the play which do not seem to be wholly accounted for on the grounds that it is the expression of a frustrated libidinous drive. Why, for example, is Hamlet so hard with Ophelia and so filled with disgust at his mother if he really unconsciously loves them both? Their unfaithfulness to him, it is true, accounts for some of his reactions, but is hardly sufficient to explain the fact that he drives Ophelia to an insane suicide. Then, too, the tremendous force of Hamlet's aggression against the father image does not seem adequately accounted for as a mere internalization of an external social or individual impression. But if aggression is just as much inherent in the psyche as libido, how does it fit into the structure of the psyche? To this Freud had an answer in his theory of psychic levels or stages of regression. The earliest of these levels he had named the oral level because at this stage in the infant's life the chief contact with reality is through the lips, mouth, and throat. At this time the child's chief external object of interest is the mother whose breast or bottle provides it with nourishment. An intermediate level of regression was designated as anal to signify that during this period the child is concerned with pleasure derived from the functions of excretion. A third level was described as oedipal, phallic, or genital, and it is here that the child becomes preoccupied with his or her relation to the father image. The oedipus complex whether considered in its aggressive or libidinous aspects, is therefore not an isolated phenomenon in the psyche. It has a long history, the roots of which are to be found on the oral level of the child's experience.[4]

If we examine the nature of this earliest conflict situation with which the child has to struggle on the oral level of experience we can soon see how the basic drives involved acquire their specific character. In the first few months of life the child is wholly dependent on the mother for nourishment and care. Unfortunately, however, it does not fully realize at first that the mother is an independent being with other interests than "his majesty's" comfort. It still thinks of the mother as part of its own world as was the case, indeed, during the intra-uterine existence. Due to this basic confusion as to the extent to which it has its environment under control, the child is likely to react naively and emotionally to any one of the inevitable frustrations which will occur to it. A temporary refusal of the breast is interpreted by the child as an irrevocable loss of part of its own body—the part which supplies it with the all-essential nourishment. It is not surprising that the first reaction to such experiences should be a feeling of complete passivity, of abandonment to a hostile world. Nevertheless the child's organism is not so easily frightened as his psyche. It soon forces the psyche to react aggressively, to exert some sort of effort to acquire the much-needed breast which it has lost. Unfortunately here, too, the child is at a disadvantage. It is motorically helpless and can only express its efforts to retrieve the lost part of its world emotionally. But the important point is that the child's earliest experiences of emotional passivity and aggression are centered around the breast and the mother who the child gradually learns is the possessor of the breast.

This fact is of peculiar significance for the writer and hence for the analysis of the literary works which he produces. The original analytic theory assumed that the creative writer expresses his repressed unconscious wishes in a disguised form. On the basis of thirty-six analyzed cases of practicing writers, Dr. Edmund Bergler, a former director of the Vienna Psychoanalytic Clinic, contradicted this assumption. He maintained that the writer expresses only *defenses* against repressed conflicts. He held that a writer is a chronic defendant accused before the tribunal of his unconscious conscience. It accuses him of one "crime," namely: unresolved masochistic attachment to the image of his mother. This attachment Bergler denominated the "breast complex" which implies both the extreme passivity of the child with respect to the breast and also the tendency to take pleasure in the pain of this submission and refusal. To counteract the indictment of the unconscious conscience the writer produces a peculiar alibi: he denies the mere existence of the mother. In the process of productivity, he establishes a materialization of the "autarchic fantasy": he acts unconsciously *both* roles, that of the "giving mother" and the "recipient child." He gives himself, out of himself, beautiful words and ideas. He does this by the identification of words and milk and thus he denies both his original dependence on the mother and the later masochistic elaboration of that dependence.

Dr. Bergler thus considers writing a "self-curative alibi sickness." This alibi compulsion leads to the well-known fact that the writer is a chronic rebel. Whether he attacks institutions, mores, or prejudices, he does so primarily, from the unconscious point of view, to prove to himself that he is aggressive and not passive to mother. But this aggression is only pseudo-aggression, covering deep masochistic attachment. The title of the present book, for example, is taken from the dream poem *Kubla Khan* wherein Coleridge characterizes the Romantic poet as aggressive to the point of being demonic. This was and is a common conception of the Romantics, particularly Byron, Shelley, and Keats. But biographical evidence and analysis of typical poems do not bear out this conception. These poets were unconsciously highly passive people always struggling to hold their own in a world which more normal people took in their stride, but to which the Romantics succumbed.

According to Dr. Bergler there is a third alibi, also unconsciously provided for in this battle of the conscience. It involves a shifting of the guilt which rightfully pertains to psychic masochism and a crediting of this guilt to the defensive aggression. This is a sort of taking the blame for the lesser crime. The fourth and final alibi of the writer pertains to scopophilia, the voyeuristic tendency to peep, and its exhibitionistic opposite, to show off. The writer is an exquisite voyeur who is capable of sublimating his voyeurism into what is known as "imagination." Under the pressure of his inner conscience his peeping is changed into exhibitionism and thus by producing his writings and publishing them the writer exhibits before the reader. Once more he is taking the blame for the lesser crime. Dr. Bergler's opinions on writers are part of his work on oral regression and psychic masochism. He claims that the role of unconscious conscience has been underestimated. He also advances the idea that every neurosis has an oral basis, though there are many rescue stations from the oral danger.

The oral and gustatory sensations, then, which the child reacts to are confused and identified in his gradually developing psyche with auditory and visual sensations, and since these latter sensations are to be the foundations of the child's ability to use words, it is clear that his use of words may become subject to these same extremes of passivity and aggression which were impressed upon his early oral sensations. It is further important for the child's later ability to use words that his earliest associations of the sensations out of which they are formed should be in connection with the mother. For in the case of the writer the confusion of these earliest sensations has led to the unconscious identification of words and milk. Since the the child's earliest experience of both is received from the mother its reactions to both will be similar. If the child feels that mother is refusing milk, he may in later life feel unconsciously that his unconscious mother image is refusing words-milk. In the case of the writer this lack is remedied by the attempt to supply himself with words-milk and hence dispense with the recalcitrant mother image.[5] This unconscious reaction to an unconscious need goes a long way toward explaining the writer's compulsive productivity. But it should be noted that this compulsive giving of words to himself is the result of the writer's infantile conflict with the mother image. It is based on a primary masochistic passivity in which the infant feels abandoned with respect to its source of nourishment and a specific defensive and aggressive reaction which tries to overcome this passivity by denying the need for the mother's breast and substituting one's own power to give words-milk.

If the above theory as to the writer's unconscious motivation is correct, it is clear that any analysis of the unconscious fantasies which he expresses in his work must give primary attention to those elements which indicate his passivity before the mother image and the various aggressive defenses with which he seeks to compensate for passivity. It is also clear that libidinous tendencies will be of interest, but only of secondary interest because the writer's basic reaction to love objects of the opposite sex is one of conflict and frustration rather than possible gratification. If we return to our analysis of Hamlet we can now find an answer to the question of why Hamlet's unconscious love for Ophelia and Gertrude should express itself in such extreme hatred and aggression. Shakespeare is not expressing his own unconscious oedipus conflict directly, he is using it as a defense for his more deeply rooted oral conflict with the mother. He has succeeded in shifting most of his oral aggression against the mother image to the father, but not quite all. What is left accounts for the not quite typically oedipal treatment of Gertrude and Ophelia. Moreover, if some of Shakespeare's sonnets can be taken as evidence of his, perhaps unconscious, homosexual tendencies we have a strong proof of the supposition that he could not be motivated by a frustrated unconscious libidinous attachment to the mother image. For male homosexuals are unconsciously motivated by a violent rejection of the mother image, and hence all women, with a consequent conscious preference for male lovers exclusively.

Another example may make this point more clear, for Shakespeare's *Hamlet* is such a perfect oedipal defense that it is very difficult to prove conclusively that there is a still deeper conflict present in it. Moreover, since we have no definite proof of Shakespeare's homosexuality we cannot depend on this as an indication of an unconscious oral conflict with the mother image. But these uncertainties do not attend what seems to be the parallel case of Sophocles' *Oedipus Rex*. In this play, from which Freud drew his name for the oedipus conflict, the hero displays no aggressive tendencies toward his mother at all. All his aggression is concentrated on the father whom he has killed, and his libido is fully gratified in his subsequent unwitting incest with his mother. Does this mean, then, that Sophocles was expressing an unconscious attachment to his mother? This is hardly possible for it is a biographical fact that Sophocles was a confirmed homosexual and this implies an unconscious hatred of the mother image.[6] Moreover he could not become conscious of his own oedipus complex as he clearly was. It is clear then that Sophocles must have been using his version of the oedipus story as a disguise or defense for his true unconscious conflict with the mother. There is an indication of this unconscious hatred in the play when he makes Jocasta commit suicide upon hearing of the crime of incest of which she and her son are guilty. Her suicide is by hanging as Gertrude's, in *Hamlet*, is by poison, to symbolize the basic oral conflict.

In the studies of the romantic poems which are to follow we shall have occasion to cite further examples of the defensive use of the oedipus complex. It is sufficient to note here the possibility of the writer's shifting his early aggressive tendencies against the mother to the father. In this shift the frightening mother of pregenital infancy is demoted and the father seemingly takes over as an object for the child's aggression. The original passivity to the mother remains but the child manages to deny it by saying that he is not afraid of mother but that father is the real object of his fear. His reason for doing so is that no unconscious conflict is ever static. If the psyche is dominated by an infantile fear of the mother image it will try to escape that fear by denying the existence of its object. The shifting of the original aggression from mother to father is part of this denial. There are, however, other defenses which may be employed to escape from the original source of conflict. We note a few of these briefly so that we may see some of the basic unconscious patterns which writers may express.

Besides the positive oedipus complex, of which there are many examples besides the *Oedipus Rex* and *Hamlet,* there is the negative oedipus complex. In this pattern the aggression which was shifted from mother to father undergoes a further change. It is turned against the self with the result that the child can deny that he is aggressive toward either parent. The aggression which he has turned against himself is now invested in masochism whereby he is identified with the mother image and submits to what he takes to be the father sadistic attacks on the mother. The feminine identification which is typical of the negative oedipus complex gives rise to what is known as "spurious" homosexuality. This type differs from perversion homosexuality in that the level of regression on which it is based is not so deep as in the case of true orally regressed homosexuality. The basic oral conflict with the mother is apparent, however, in that it is the mother image which is attacked even while the patient thinks that he has escaped from his submission to it. This pattern too will be illustrated in some of the romantic works which we are to examine.

Another unconscious defensive pattern which writers express in their works is the homosexual fantasy. In this fantasy there is no attempt to shift the conflict with the pre-oedipal mother image onto the oedipal or genital level. The patient has understandably no real interest in genital sexuality because his conflict arose at a time when genital interests were not yet awakened. His defense therefore takes the form of a direct rejection of the mother image and of heterosexuality. This direct aggression is expressed in consciousness by a preference for male (or female, as the case may be) lovers and a consequent rejection of the opposite sex. The use of this defense is indicative of a much more serious conflict than that indicated by the oedipal defense. For the latter has a certain amount of stability insofar as it implies a pseudo-acceptance of heterosexuality. But in the homosexual defense the aggression is so violent that it approaches a complete rejection of women. It is not surprising, therefore, that society regards homosexuality as a reprehensible perversion.[7] It is in connection with the homosexual fantasy that still another fantasy is important: that of the phallic mother. The phallic mother is to be clearly distinguished from the oedipal mother. The former is a much more terrible image and stems from the pregenital level of experience. The latter is typically passive and ineffectual since on this level the father is the real object of fear. It is indeed this fantasy which seems to be at the basis of the homosexual tendency. The child, in this instance, reacts to frustrations at the breast by searching on its own body for a substitute breast. This it finds in its urinary apparatus which, like the breast, is a dispenser of liquid. This new conception of the breast may now be projected back upon the mother image and the result, in the case of the male child, is the mother with the penis. It is this feminine image which the adult may seek as a love object in later life and the result is that he tends to make a homosexual choice.

Still another type of defense on the oral level involves a projection of the already defensive aggression onto the mother image, thus making it responsible for the child's passivity in a double sense. This defense is expressed in several different ways. For instance there is the fantasy that the mother's breast is the source of poisonous nourishment. This fantasy seems to be at the bottom of chronic drunkenness. Or perhaps the breast is conceived of as the source of a destructive flood and hence death by water results. Then there is the fantasy that the mother is a devouring monster— clearly a projection of the child's own biting tendencies. Or there may be a general assumption that the mother is in the wrong and a consequent acting out—by means of what is termed a magic gesture—of how the patient would like to have been treated or, perhaps, would not like to have been treated. This way of putting the blame on the other person can be directed at either parent, but its aggressive nature should not be overlooked. Further we may note that cynicism is a technique whereby the devaluation of the patient's own ego, which has taken place as a result of long-continued inner conflict, is projected outward onto various representatives of authority. There it is attacked with the same severity with which the patient's inner conscience attacks his defeated ego. A similar defensive use of aggression is evident in other kinds of satire. Finally we may note that regression to the anal stage of psychic development may also be used defensively. The child's forbidden wishes to retain and play with feces are really aggressive defenses against the passive experiences involved in defecating and urinating. The later sublimation of these experiences in the heaping up of wealth are similar defenses against a basic passivity.

There are two other pairs of general tendencies which are frequently expressed in literature. The first of these is masochism as a particular type of passivity and its aggressive defense, sadism. Masochism implies the tendency to submit to some authority and accept pain as if it were pleasure. In the realms of the unconscious this authority may be either a mother or father image; however, since the child's earliest experience of passivity and submission is in relation to the mother it is clear that masochistic submission will appear most frequently on the oral level. If this is the case, the artist will sometimes portray women in the role of the sadist and thus project his own aggressive defense onto the object to which he submits. In other instances the sadistic defense may not be projected, but be used to cover the patient's masochistic tendencies. It is an established fact that some authors have been perverted masochists (e.g., Dr. Johnson and Swinburne), just as it is known that others have been homosexuals, drunkards, or drug addicts: all symptoms which point to the generalization that psychologically there is an oral conflict involved. But most of the tendencies to masochism which we will observe in the romantic works which we are to analyze will be examples of psychic masochism as opposed to perverted masochism. This more subtle form of masochism is more likely to appear in literature on account of the numerous ways in which such psychic masochism may be disguised. It may appear as asceticism sanctioned and promoted by religion. It may appear in the form of wholly unexpected catastrophe which has nevertheless been unconsciously provoked. In any case the tendency to bring suffering on the self will always be apparent.

The other pair of neurotic tendencies which are expressed in literary works are exhibitionism and voyeurism. The latter, which seems to be the more basic tendency, is akin to the oral wish to get and take in. Thus the voyeur uses his eyes to take in forbidden sights just as the lips are used to suck at the breast. The frustration of this attempt to take in sights leads to the defense which says: I do not want to take in—look at, I want to give out—show off. In the case of the writer this exhibitionistic defense is one of the motivations for his putting his fantasies on paper and his publication of them. Thus in many cases writers will seem to be revealing more about themselves than they actually are, for their apparent need to "wear their hearts upon their sleeves" is only a defense against a deeper desire to play the voyeur. But here again the artist's exhibitionism is also an attempt at self-cure, an attempt to give himself the sights which others deny him.

In this brief sketch of psychoanalytic theory we have indicated some of the unconscious patterns and tendencies which may be found in works of literature. We thus have some idea of what we are looking for. We may now take up the discussion of what sort of evidence can be adduced for the presence of these unconscious fantasies. Perhaps the first suggestion that comes to mind is that since we are interpreting an author's work in the light of his personal experience, we should therefore rely heavily on biographical data. This however is not the case. In the first place the available evidence on even the best-documented authors, living or dead, is still so meager that it is of little value for the subtle purposes of psychoanalysis. At best it can only be used as corroborating evidence for an examination of the author's literary works. For it is here alone, as in dreams, that we have anything approaching direct access to the writer's unconscious. The observations of his contemporaries, his own autobiographical reflections, his letters, etc., are all likely to be altered and distorted by conscious predispositions. But in his creative work the author is most firmly under the control of his "muse," and here, as in dreams, he is most likely to reveal his unconscious tendencies most plainly. It appears then that the evidence for our interpretations of literary works must be found within the works themselves. It is for this reason, as stated before, that detailed analysis is indispensable.

On what basis does this analysis proceed? The theory, of course, is useful as a guide in determining what we must look for, but it cannot be used as proof if we are concerned with proving the presence of these very theoretical patterns. We must resort to more particular items of evidence for proof. The most important of these is the precise interpretation we are to put upon the symbols employed in the work. It is true that symbols often admit of a wide latitude in meaning and this means that no interpretation, including those in this book, can claim infallibility, but as Freud has remarked in *Interpretation of Dreams,* there are limits beyond which we cannot stretch the significance of any particular symbol. A stick can hardly be used to symbolize the feminine genitals, nor a ring the male. Some symbols therefore seem to be naturally appropriate to what they symbolize. Others are partially determined by cultural factors. Thus the earth, the moon, the sea, and Nature personified have long been recognized as mother symbols due to their feminine personifications in classical mythology. Similarly the sun has long been personified as a male god who is an archer. This latter detail is particularly appropriate to the fact that the child at the breast is motorically helpless and hence must direct his aggression at the mother from a distance. On the other hand, stars, insofar as they may be thought of as closely related to the moon, may symbolize the child's constant devotion to the inconstant mother.

In view of the fact that the breast complex seems to be of primary importance to the writer and thus likely to find frequent expression in literature, it may be worthwhile to note some of the more frequently used symbols in the complex. Domes, mountains, pyramids, and cups by their mere shape are suggestive of the breast. Streams, fountains, and floods can be used to symbolize it as the source of liquid nourishment, just as apples and food in general may also be associated with this same aspect. A more complicated symbol for the child at the breast is the tree, which insofar as it sucks liquid from mother earth in the spring, breathes through its leaves all summer long, and is drained of its sap in the fall has definite oral connotations. Birds, however, seem to be the most frequent symbols for the breast in Romantic literature and this at first seems difficult to understand, especially in view of the fact that flying has some associations with sexual intercourse and that bird and penis are sometimes identified. Nevertheless, compared to most animals, birds are not easy to distinguish sexually—differences in color being negligible for the child in this respect. This makes them good symbols for the presexual emotions of the breast complex. They also come and go with inexplicable suddenness and this may symbolize the fact that the child has no control over the comings and goings of the breast. Especially important for poets is the fact that birds are among the few species of animals which express their emotions in compulsive song—a valuable detail in the unconscious symbolization of the identification words-milk.[8]

Most of the other symbols which appear in poetry are familiar to readers of Freud's *Interpretation of Dreams*. In addition to these we may note that the pregenital fantasy of the devouring mother often symbolizes the mother as cat, tiger, lioness, or sphinx. The fantasy of the phallic mother is symbolized in the image of the Lamia, or snake woman, and sometimes the dragon represents the phallic breast. On the genital level flowers seem to be a fairly consistent symbol for heterosexuality. This is no doubt due to the easily observed fact that flowers are pollinated by insects who enter the blossom in symbolic coitus. Furthermore, flowers have the advantage of being objects of great beauty which thus makes possible a sublimation of what seem to the neurotic the grosser aspects of sexual intercourse. The fact that they cannot approach each other may also be one of these mitigating factors. (Spengler thought this fact one of the most tragic aspects of life!) Since, however, most poets seem only to use the genital level of experience as a disguise or defense for their interest in earlier levels of regression, the choice of symbols on the genital level is less rich and revealing than it is on the earlier oral and anal levels.

The precise interpretation of symbols and the detection of the basic unconscious patterns which have been discovered in clinical psychoanalysis are the chief types of internal evidence upon which we can rely. One other rule is worth noting as an aid in ensuring accuracy of interpretation. This is that no part of the work under consideration should be omitted from the interpretation as insignificant or meaningless. It is often the case that the clue to an interpretation lies in passages whose relevance we cannot at first grasp. True, the mere fact that we can attach some meaning to every portion of the work will not ensure the completeness of the interpretation. Other more fundamental meanings may still be overlooked. Nevertheless, the chances that this will happen are fewer where a complete and coherent interpretation is attempted. There is also a sense in which any full and coherent interpretation of work of art has value regardless of the truth or falsity of the scientific data on which it rests. Psychoanalysis, as we now know it, may be totally revised in the future, but if it can contribute meaningful interpretations of works of art in its present state, it has real value. In the same way the Song of Solomon is more meaningful for the elaborate medieval mystical interpretations of it—even though we know that such interpretations are not the most historical or even authoritative.

This brings us to a statement of the value of psychoanalytical interpretation of literature. Assuming that the psychoanalytical theory employed is scientifically true, I believe that the primary value of such interpretation, in addition to making the work more understandable and meaningful, is to determine the strength and completeness of the defenses against more deeply repressed conflicts which the work of art is intended to disguise. These defenses had value for the artist and are presumably his chief unconscious motive in composing his work. They also have value for readers of the work inasmuch as they too are in need of similar defenses. Thus, for example, *Hamlet* may be considered a very nearly perfect oedipal defense for the more deeply repressed oral conflict, and this may, in fact, account in part for its great popularity over several centuries. Similarly, some of the appeal of Byron's and of Shelley's poetry, over that of Coleridge or Keats, may be due to their both employing the negative oedipal defense as opposed to Coleridge's and Keats' more direct confronting of the oral conflict on the pregenital level. And Wordsworth's greater popularity than all four of these writers may be due to the fact that he avoids, for the most part, both pregenital and genital defenses and employs instead various forms of the magic gesture. Such a criterion, however, is dependent on a recognition of the fact that the value which we set on a work of art is partially determined by the extent to which we can use it for our own unconscious purposes.

But we may wish to employ other criteria. One such would involve the fact that the artist who has the completest insight into the unconscious, will, intuitively, create works of the most value. Here psychoanalytic interpretation is obviously indispensable for we cannot tell what intuitive insight the artist has been capable of without the more discursive reasoning of psychoanalysis. The results of the application of such a criterion would be different from that of the previous criterion. Here Coleridge is indubitably a more interesting poet than Wordsworth. And Byron, Shelley, and Keats are perhaps even more rewarding than either of the two earlier poets. This may be because they could profit from the insights of their predecessors and were consequently less hampered by the inhibiting force of convention. But valuable as psychoanalysis may be, it should be remembered that psychological meaning in a work of art is only a part of its total meaning and hence cannot claim to offer any absolute standard of judgment. Moreover, the application of psychoanalytic technique to any work cannot pretend to give even the total psychological content of the work. Many aspects on the conscious level must be overlooked and held in the background in order to see it through the analytic microscope. It is sufficient if the microscope reveals something of the immensity of the work which we had not known before and which we can see to be both valuable and true.

It should not, moreover, be forgotten when we come to consider the analysis of individual works that a delineation of the unconscious elements contained in them in no way destroys or minimizes the conscious values for which they have long been famed. All of the poems analyzed in this book are acknowledged masterpieces whose beauty and literary excellence will continue to fascinate readers for years to come even if their unconscious meanings are known. Still, as a consequence, some readers may feel considerable disappointment and even resentment at learning that some of the poems have unconscious meanings which seem at variance with their better-known conscious meanings. Such resentment, however, I believe is unjustified. The greatness of great poetry is not diminished by learning its unconscious foundations. On the contrary, we now can see how its imperishable ideals are rooted in an equally solid base. The same attitude is worth recommending with regard to psychoanalytic interpretations of the facts of an author's biography. Public opinion is rapidly becoming more and more enlightened on these matters. Statistical studies, for example, have made us familiar with the fact that a much larger percentage of males have homosexual experiences than was hitherto supposed. This in turn may make it easier for us to understand that writers must occasionally express homosexual fantasies in their work. In the nineteenth century people were shocked at the rumors that Byron had incestuous relations with his sister, or that Keats' love for Fanny Brawne had a strong element of perversion in it. Today we can understand that such facts are not matter for moral condemnation alone. They are clues to the understanding of the writer and his work.

II

COLERIDGE

Christabel, Part I • *The Ancient Mariner*
Christabel, Part II

COLERIDGE'S *Christabel* has long been an enigma to commentators. There is, for example, Fanny Godwin's statement that "Lamb says 'Christabel' ought never to have been published, and that no one understands it." Yet the fascination which the poem exercised over its readers from the start was remarkable. Even before its publication it was well known and praised, and its fame has not diminished since. Efforts have, of course, been made to render it more intelligible by tracking down its sources and fitting these into a mosaic of meaning. But the results have been generally unsatisfying. It has been ascertained that Coleridge was interested in the tradition of the Gothic romance at the time he wrote the poem, but this tells us little for the psychological structure of the Gothic tale is itself in need of explanation. Thus puzzling questions still remain. The major ones are, I think: Who are Christabel and Geraldine? What is their relation to each other? And what meaning do they give to the poem as a whole? On the surface the story does not present an answer to these questions. And yet they are problems which demand an answer, for without them we are at a loss to see why a half-finished, medieval tale about a vampire and an innocent maid should interest so many people for so long.

It may help to give a brief statement of the situation involved. Christabel is betrothed to her absent lover, but she cannot sleep for thinking of him and on this account she wanders late at night in the wood near her father's castle. Here she meets Geraldine who is to exercise such an evil influence over her. The rest of the first part of the poem is scarcely more than an unfolding of this evil influence as the two women pass within the castle and spend the night together in Christabel's bedroom. But the paucity of action only increases the difficulty of identifying the relations of the two main characters to each other.

There are several reasons why we cannot take Geraldine as someone wholly unrelated and unknown to Christabel prior to this time. Aside from the fact that a good deal of dramatic intensity is lost by introducing such an extraneous character, there is no conscious motivation for Geraldine's actions toward Christabel. The idea that Christabel as pure innocence (the pun on Christ and Christabel is adduced in favor of this theory) must be made to suffer for the sins of others, and therefore Geraldine is needed as the instrument of her suffering, seems to have little support in the text of the poem. A variant of this theory has been proposed wherein Christabel's sufferings are compared to those of St. Teresa. Thus "what both Teresa and Christabel are desirous of achieving would be a test of love, through admiration of the loved one, but where Teresa's is a purely spiritual love, Christabel's is a sexual (albeit 'romantic') love for her knight."[1] It does not seem to me, however, that Coleridge has stressed the theme of sexual love in the text of the poem. Christabel's lover is mentioned at the beginning and then forgotten. We never hear about him from her lips and there is no suggestion that Geraldine's function is to ruin Christabel's chances with her knight. As we shall see the poem really seems to have less to do with love than with hate. Furthermore, this association of Christabel with the suffering Christ does not avoid the necessity of supposing that Geraldine represents something more than just an evil witch or vampire. On this assumption Geraldine must represent Satan or evil personified, and then we must ask why Coleridge insisted on making such an abstraction assume the character of a woman and why her persecutions take the form they do.

But if we reject the suggestion that Geraldine is merely a personification of Satan, what other suggestions remain? P. G. Patmore is supposed to have told Rossetti that it was common gossip in Coleridge's day that Geraldine was to turn out to be Christabel's absent lover. This possibility is worth considering since it would fit in with the fact that Christabel's thoughts are occupied with her lover when she meets Geraldine. But there is a good deal that remains unexplained on this assumption too. We should want to know, for example, why Christabel is so horrified at the sight of Geraldine when she disrobes in the bed chamber. Then, too, why should Geraldine as Christabel's lover exercise such a spell over her and at the same time, in the second part of the poem, gain the complete confidence of the father? We should expect quite the opposite from her lover under these circumstances. Finally there would be the evidence of an important passage in the poem which, far from hinting that Geraldine is Christabel's lover in disguise, states directly that she is Christabel's mother. This, indeed, presents a third possibility as to what Geraldine means to Christabel. We shall presently examine the evidence which the text offers for this hypothesis, but here we may note that the ballad from which Coleridge derived Christabel's name has a Geraldine-like character who bewitches her young stepdaughter in a forest scene which reminds us of the opening scene of Coleridge's poem. The first two stanzas of the ballad read as follows:

> *My father was an aged knight*
> *And yet it chanced so,*
> *He took to wife a false lady,*
> *Which brought me to this woe.*
> *She witched me, being a fair young maid,*
> *In the green forest to dwell;*
> *And there to abide in loathly shape,*
> *Most like a fiend in hell.*

If we suppose, tentatively, that Geraldine is unconsciously meant to represent Christabel's mother, we are at least a little closer to being able to fit the poem into a background of biographical data (to be discussed later) which we have from Coleridge's life. Geraldine as Satan or the absent lover would hardly be so meaningful to Coleridge from the unconscious point of view as Geraldine as mother. But this equation suggests the further possibility that Christabel may herself represent someone in Coleridge's experience. It is, perhaps, unwise to assume that in every literary work the author must identify himself with one or any of the characters. Yet the poet like the dreamer is unconsciously preoccupied with his personal problems, even though consciously he may strive to be more objective. There is at least a likelihood that this has been the case in *Christabel* if we consider the importance which Coleridge attached to the poem. Thus he might easily have identified himself with Christabel, if with anyone in the poem, since she has the most important role in the action. In any event, the association would be valid on the grounds that the mother-daughter relation is basically a mother-child relation, and reasons will soon be apparent why Coleridge would want to disguise his childhood relationship to his mother by changing the sex of his protagonist.

Before we attempt to substantiate these guesses as to the identity of Geraldine and Christabel, there is one other element in the poem which must be made clear before we can have a working hypothesis for its interpretation. This element is the precise character of the mother-child relationship which we have assumed to exist between Geraldine and Christabel. On the surface, Geraldine seems to be a bad mother insofar as she exercises an evil spell over Christabel. But how can we describe Geraldine's "badness" in terms which will have the sort of universal significance which can reasonably be expected from the poem? The closest Coleridge himself came to stating this relationship is his remark on some lines from Crashaw's *The Tears of St. Teresa*. The lines are:

> Since 'tis not to be had at home
> She'd travel to a martyrdom.

Coleridge is said to have remarked that these lines "were ever present to the Second Part of 'Christabel'—if, indeed, by some subtle process of mind they did not suggest the first thought of the entire poem." The remark is in itself cryptic, since we do not see at first glance why Christabel should be considered a martyr to the wiles of Geraldine. Teresa's martyrdom for Christ had meaning in terms of the mystical theology which formed its background. But the annihilation of the earthly self in order to obtain union with the heavenly Christ is certainly not part of Coleridge's intention for Christabel with her earthly lover. If this were the case we should expect some mention in the text to make clear this purpose of Christabel's suffering. There is none so far as I can see. However, our assumption of a mother-child relationship does not, at first, seem to throw any more light on the problem. The relationship between child and mother seems hardly to bear any resemblance to that between martyr and persecutor, which Coleridge says is important.

It will be of some assistance at this point to strip the term "martyrdom" of its theological implications (which are, however, important for other aspects of the poem) and to consider it solely from a psychological point of view. Thus regarded it has definite associations with the phenomena of sadism and masochism. The martyr, from the common-sense point of view, is, to some extent, a masochist in that he accepts punishment which less scrupulous persons might adroitly avoid. Likewise, the persecutor is a sadist, at least from the martyr's point of view, insofar as the tortures he inflicts are for crimes which the martyr does not acknowledge. There is thus the suspicion that both martyr and persecutor in some cases derive a certain amount of unconscious pleasure from the pains which they accept and inflict, respectively. Furthermore, psychiatric research has discovered a number of interesting facts concerning masochism which not only throw considerable light upon the main theme of *Christabel* as stated by Cole ridge, also upon certain character traits in Coleridge himself which have been noted by his biographers. It has been shown by Freud, for example, in his *Beyond the Pleasure Principle* and *Civilization and Its Discontents*, that masochism, with its correlative sadism, is one of the basic elements in many neuroses and that the understanding of this element involves the understanding of large areas of character maladjustment.[2] Purely descriptive literary studies such as Mario Praz' *Romantic Agony* have also shown the importance of sadism and masochism in nineteenth-century literature. Coleridge's intuitive insight into "the facts of mind" could have glimpsed the implications of this deeply rooted human trait.

In order to understand how the mother-child relation in *Christabel* is characterized and determined by psychic masochism (as distinguished from perverted masochism) we must examine some of the theories as to its origin in the mind of the child. There is, for example, the theory that some psychic masochistic traits arise in a peculiar relationship which the child bears to its mother. According to this theory, psychic masochism is rooted in the earliest stages of infantile development. The frustrations to which the child is inevitably subject from the time of its birth are the raw material out of which the masochistic tendencies are developed. When the child tries to master these frustrations with aggressive reactions, he is naturally reprimanded for his aggressions by those in authority over him. A typical situation is that of the nursing infant who reacts aggressively to the withdrawal of the mother's breast during the weaning period. Now in the case of the child whose oral desires are particularly strongly determined in such a situation, the attempt is made to maintain those desires and at the same time to accommodate the self to the external punishment or inward guilt which must necessarily accompany such aggressive desires. In this case the child comes, strangely enough, to look upon the guilt or punishment as a pleasure desirable in itself. Viewed from another standpoint it has learned to turn its own aggression against itself and become content to accept self-punishment as a pleasurable though unconscious aim in life. This paradoxical and improbable feat the child's mind seems able to accomplish, and it is on the basis of this accomplishment that psychic masochism becomes rooted in the psyche. Once these early mechanisms are fixed there is a possibility that in all later life the primal error of confusing pain with pleasure will be pursued. Such a confusion means that the individual will unconsciously provoke situations in which he can achieve his unconscious desire for pain-pleasure. And since in most cases this confusion is earliest associated with the mother, it is clear why the mother-child relationship may be conceived as a masochistic one.

There are many difficult points in *Christabel* which gain added meaning in the light of the hypothesis we have just elaborated. The poem opens with a weird allusion to the sound which the hooting owls make at midnight. It is related that Coleridge in reciting the poem liked particularly to linger over the oral sensations aroused by these sounds. But it should be remembered that the owl, in addition to being a bird of ill omen (as the albatross turns out to be in *The Ancient Mariner*), is also the symbol of the goddess Athena, a lady whose virginity by no means mitigates her warlike cruelty, as displayed, for example, in the *Iliad*.

A similar allusion to the bad-mother image may be contained in the famous disputed passage:

> *Sir Leoline, the baron rich,*
> *Hath a toothless mastiff bitch;*

The controversy which developed over the word "bitch" shows the importance which it had for Coleridge's unconscious. For perhaps the most important unconscious association with this word is the vulgar curse word "son-of-a-bitch" which is an explicit statement of the bad mother-child relationship. Perhaps on this account Coleridge yielded to the solicitations of his friends to change, in the first edition at least, the lines to read as follows:

> *Sir Leoline, the baron rich,*
> *Hath a toothless mastiff which*
> *From her kennel beneath the rock*
> *Maketh answer to the clock.*

But it should be noted that this is not necessarily an improvement over the first reading. For "which" sounds much like "witch," and this, from the unconscious point of view, is an even more precise and common designation for the bad mother. For the infantile mind projects its own ravenous oral desires on the mother and hence creates the prototype of the witch of fairy tale lore who, in *Hänsel and Gretel* for example, eats little children alive. The deadly aspect of mother as destroyer may also be hinted at in the concluding verses of this paragraph:

> *Sixteen short howls, not over loud;*
> *Some say, she sees my lady's shroud.*

One thinks of dog-headed Scylla in the *Odyssey* with her faint, piping yelp, devouring Odysseus's men.

The moonlight in which the poem is bathed, and which for many readers has constituted one of the strongest elements in its fascination, is also apparently involved in some sort of ambivalent mother symbolism. The classical significance of the moon as goddess who watches over childbirth would not, of course, be unknown to Coleridge and is perhaps suggested by the following passage:

> *The moon is behind, and at the full;*
> *And yet she looks both small and dull.*

As a full moon it must symbolize mother in her benign aspect, but its smallness and dullness suggest an ominous influence. For she should properly give the light which she denies and this typifies her as a bad, denying mother. Even the classical idea of the moon contained this ambivalence, for she was considered under a benevolent aspect as Lucina and under a malevolent aspect as Hecate. Certainly the waxing of the moon as paralleled by the coming of spring is not in the ascendant, for Coleridge tells us that "The spring comes slowly up this way."

It is perhaps too much to suppose that Coleridge was possessed of the erudition which makes Mr. Robert Graves tell us that the oak was sacred to the White Goddess in one of her most venerable forms.[3] But Coleridge's phrase about the "huge, broad-breasted, old oak tree" seems to foreshadow the horror which Geraldine's bosom is to inspire in Christabel. It is also curious that Christabel should be driven outside the castle to pray under the oak in consequence of her bad dreams about her lover. (A struggle with one or the other of the infantile parent images is particularly apropos at this time since the child frequently misconceives parental influence as forbidding all pleasure, including that which accompanies sexual love.) It is, of course, convenient that Christabel should wander in the wood so she may discover Geraldine there, but there is a possibility that in leaving the castle Christabel is symbolically rejecting the mother image represented, as is common in dreams, by the castle. If this is the case, Christabel's taking Geraldine to her room and giving her shelter is really a defense against, an attempt to deny, a still more basic rejection of the mother image. On this supposition Christabel's prayer is an attempt to placate the already aggrieved mother image. Perhaps, too, the midnight walk in the wood and the mention of the mistletoe on the oak have overtones meaning to suggest Aeneas' descent into the underworld insofar as it symbolizes an encounter with the more terrifying aspects of mother earth.

Another passage which seems to have had special significance for Coleridge, since it is noted in Dorothy Wordsworth's *Journal* at the time of the composition of the poem, is:

> *The one red leaf, the last of its clan,*
> *That dances as often as dance it can,*
> *Hanging so light, and hanging so high,*
> *On the topmost twig that looks up at the sky.*

The curious detail of the red leaf in these lines may possibly be taken to suggest the helpless dependency of the child nursing at the mother's breast. This suggestion is strengthened when we compare these lines with the first three in the conclusion to Part II which we shall presently discuss. There we have a "red-cheeked child," who, like the red leaf in these lines, is pictured as singing and dancing to itself. But there the nursing condition is made more explicit in the cryptic line which describes the child as one "that always finds and never seeks." So, too, in the following paragraph of the poem the divine dyad of mother and son, Jesu and Maria, as later Mary, the mother, alone, is invoked to protect the imperiled Christabel.

The hypothesis of a conflict between mother and child, toward which all these hidden allusions seem to be pointing, may also explain to a certain extent the reason for Geraldine's fainting condition before she arrives at Christabel's bedchamber. For just as Christabel's own mother died in childbirth—that is, as a result of Christabel's aggression against her—so Geraldine was forcibly abducted by five ruffians who carried her across the "shade of night" and abandoned her more dead than alive. (Coleridge's fondness for the number five, which appears in *Kubla Khan* as "twice five" and in *The Ancient Mariner* as "four times fifty" may possibly be an allusion to the ten children which made up the Coleridge family.) The weakness of Geraldine at first, then, may represent Christabel's identification of her with her long-dead mother. But the moment Christabel speaks of the role which this dead mother played in her life, that is, she made the wildflower wine which Christabel now offers as a cordial to Geraldine, thus reversing the roles and playing the giving mother herself, at this moment the unconscious image of the denying mother breaks through and she begins to see Geraldine in the light in which she appears throughout the rest of the poem. Thus it may not be too fanciful to suppose that the shock of mentioning (i.e., giving words which are unconsciously identified by the infant with milk from the breast) the good mother, while actually confronted by the bad mother, is enough to make Christabel and Coleridge realize that only the bad-mother image is real.

In any case three important hints prepare the reader for this change of character in Geraldine. The first is that when Geraldine faints at the doorway, an act which betrays her as a bad spirit, Christabel voluntarily bears

her across the lintel and thus foreshadows the masochistic attachment from
which she later cannot free herself. Perhaps Christabel performs her good
deed precisely because she must defend herself from the charge that she
herself has rejected the bad-mother image which Geraldine is. The second
hint is the angry moan of the mastiff bitch as the two women pass the
kennel. The moan, it seems, may be directed against either Christabel or
Geraldine, or both. The important fact is that the bitch as a symbol of the
bad mother is made to appear hostile for the first time, since Coleridge says
that "never till now she uttered yell." The third hint is in the fact that the
flaring flames of the hearth as the two ladies pass light up Geraldine's eyes
and the boss on Sir Leoline's shield, an object which resembles the nipple
of a breast. It is thus an object of dread to the child with an oral conflict
and who in a voyeuristic sense "drinks" with his eyes. Sir Leoline's shield,
indeed, as that which covers and protects him, is a convenient symbol for
the mother.

The conflict which now ensues between Geraldine and the ghost of
Christabel's mother may be interpreted as a struggle between the good- and
bad-mother symbols which are vying for dominance in Christabel's (that
is Coleridge's) unconscious. From this point of view it is understandable
why Geraldine first says that she wishes Christabel's mother were present,
then drives her off when she seemingly appears. Christabel's remark that
her dead mother would appear on her wedding night may mean that this
night is to be her wedding night since the mother has actually appeared—
at least to Geraldine. But I do not believe that this supposition can be
extended to mean that Christabel is to suffer for the sake of her absent
lover. Coleridge seems to be saying that the ghost of Christabel's mother
and Geraldine are different aspects of the same ambivalent mother image,
though Geraldine is slowly winning dominance. Nevertheless Geraldine tells
Christabel that:

All they who live in the upper sky,
Do love you, holy Christabel!

Here Coleridge seems to be reassuring himself that the masochistic attachment which the child has for the mother is no fault of the real mother. And
this is largely true, since it is the child's misconception of the mother which
creates the masochistic attachment. This fact may also explain the lines in
which Geraldine seems more distressed than Christabel by the horrid em-
brace to which she is forced. In these strange lines which move from painful
nausea to scornful defiance, Coleridge says:

> *Yet Geraldine nor speaks nor stirs;*
> *Ah! what a stricken look was her's!*
> *Deep from within she seems half-way*
> *To lift some weight with sick assay,*
> *And eyes the maid and seeks delay;*
> *Then suddenly, as one defied,*
> *Collects herself in scorn and pride,*
> *And lay down by the Maiden's side!—*

The crucial passage describing what Christabel sees when Geraldine disrobes, together with the lines which were not published, is strong evidence in favor of the hypothesis that it is orally determined masochism which is troubling Coleridge and Christabel. If Geraldine were just an ordinary witch there would have been no need to center attention on her bosom, which one would expect to be less terrifying than, say, her eyes, mouth, or some other parts of her anatomy. The lines, as given in the E. H. Coleridge edition of the poem (though some editors amend the word "hidden" to "hideous") are as follows:[4]

> *Behold! her bosom and half her side—*
> *Are lean and old and foul of hue*
> *[Hidden, deformed and pale of hue*
> *A sight to dream of, not to tell!]*
> *O shield her! shield sweet Christabel!*
> *[And she is to sleep by Christabel.]*

E. H. Coleridge remarked that Hazlitt's and other contemporaries' slanderous allusions to these lines, which we have already noted as the suggestion that Geraldine was to turn into Christabel's absent knight, may well have had some basis in a remark made to him by Coleridge as to Geraldine's masculine character. In any case we can now see, in the light of our hypothesis as to the theme of oral masochism in the poem, why this rumor about Geraldine is both true and yet does not involve making her an apparition of Christabel's lover. For it seems that Christabel and Coleridge are horrified by the unconscious infantile fantasy of the phallic mother which is a part of the complex which lies at the basis of oral masochism. The fantasy arises in the mind of the child when it attempts to overcome the disappointment involved in the withdrawal of the breast. To compensate for this disappointment the male child searches on his own body for a substitute for the breast. This he finds in his own genitals which have certain obvious similarities to the breast. Once this confusion becomes established in the child's mind, the voyeuristic tendencies, whose point of likeness with the oral tendencies lies in the fact that both are impulses to take in, may lead the child to believe that the feminine genitals are similar to the male. In so doing the infantile mind reasserts its oral desires by projecting upon the woman another "breast" and at the same time satisfies the masochistic transformation of the oral tendencies by making the normal relations of the sexes impossible.[5] Women are then represented by a type found in the classic myth of Aphrodite and her associations with the mandrake, as well as many other myths (e.g., Circe) in which a "bad mother" appears bearing some sort of symbol to indicate her phallic character. It is interesting that Geraldine's name, which is the feminine of Gerald, means "spear

That Geraldine is the phallic mother is, I believe, also to be seen in the wielder " according to its Teutonic origin.

following lines where the stress is laid on the relation of the child to the mother's breast and its power of making the child a giver or denier of words, for unconsciously, as we have already noted, the child identifies words and milk which are to him the two earliest gifts he receives from the mother. In an aggressive conflict with the mother image he may attempt to refute her by denying words as she denies him milk. In later life this aggressive denial may appear as the neurotic symptom known as writer's block— a symptom from which Coleridge suffered and which he also alludes to in *The Ancient Mariner,* who is first speechless and then subject to fits of compulsive speaking. This is an important point in identifying Coleridge's personal predicament with that of Christabel and the Ancient Mariner. In these lines in which Geraldine takes Christabel in her arms, the connection between the breast and the ability to give words is explicitly stated:

> *And in her arms the maid she took,*
> *Ah wel-a-day!*
> *And with low voice and doleful look*
> *These words did say:*
> *"In the touch of this bosom there worketh a spell,*
> *Which is lord of thy utterance, Christabel! . . .*

Christabel can henceforth only express a defensive remark to the effect that she rescued Geraldine in all charity, that is, she must deny her true aggressive relationship to her from now on. It is this aggressive relation which is punished by the inability to speak, a punishment peculiarly appropriate to the poet, and which is fully comprehensible only if taken in connection with the mother-child relationship which seems to exist between Geraldine and Christabel, and which Coleridge finally asserts in explicit form in the Conclusion to the First Part of the poem where he says:

And lo! the worker of these harms,
That holds the maiden in her arms,
Seems to slumber still and mild,
As a mother with her child.

In these lines we find the culmination of the unconscious motivation of the first part of the poem. By comparing Christabel in Geraldine's arms to mother and child, Coleridge seems to be saying: "It is not true that I (Christabel) as a child wanted to be refused (masochistically) the breast and that now as an adult I seek similar refusals and disappointments; on the contrary it was mother (Geraldine) who was at fault in forcing her hideous breast upon me." Unfortunately for this alibi, Christabel's very passivity before the attack of Geraldine convicts her of the crime of masochistic passivity before the tribunal of the inner conscience. In the second part of the poem, as we shall see, Christabel changes her present innocent passivity to a highly aggressive anxiety which alienates her not only from Geraldine, but from her father as well. This aggression, however, is only defensive and needed to disprove the more basic passivity. Both attitudes are rejected by the inner conscience and punished with verbal impotence and loss of love.

There is a further interesting substantiation of the basic oral situation in the poem, though scarcely more than an unconscious slip, in the footnote which Coleridge wrote to the word "tairn" in the lines:

O Geraldine! one hour was thine—
Thou'st had thy will! By tairn and rill,
The night-birds all that hour were still.

The footnote is in part as follows: "Tairn is properly a large pool or reservoir in the mountains, commonly the feeder of some mere in the valleys. Tarn Watling and Blellum Tarn, though on lower ground, are yet not exceptions, for both are on elevations and Blellum Tarn feeds the Wynander Mere." Now if we take into account the pun on the word "mere" with the French word for mother, we see that for some reason Coleridge thinks it important to acquaint his readers with the slightly irrelevant fact that small mountain pools (tairns) feed larger lowland lakes (meres). But that there may be an identification with the mother-child relationship here is hinted by the fact that Coleridge notes two exceptions to his rule that tairns "feed" meres. The exception of Tarn Watling is important, for not only does it not feed a mere, according to Coleridge, but it is the site of the castle in "The Marriage of Sir Gawaine," the ballad from which Christabel got her name, and in which the giant who overcomes the champion Arthur lives.

The symbolism of the giant (erect penis) and his conquest again reminds us of the relation between phallic symbolism and the breast complex. It looks as if, in this note, Coleridge was again intent on reversing the roles. "Not mother feeds me, I (the tairn) feed her (the mere)"!

To return to the theme of martyrdom and psychic masochism, we find it explicitly stated in the following lines from the Conclusion to the first part of the poem where Christabel is described as a youthful ascetic:

> *And oft the while she seems to smile*
> *As infants at a sudden light!*
> *Yea, she doth smile, and she doth weep,*
> *Like a youthful hermitess,*
> *Beauteous in a wilderness,*
> *Who, praying always, prays in sleep.*

It should be noted that there is no mention here, where we should expect it most, of Christabel's knight and lover—another reason for thinking that she is not suffering *for* this knight. It seems indeed that Christabel is dreaming of the breast again, for the sudden light (via the association milk-words-knowledge-light) reminds her of what she does not want and yet pretends to want. But it is of interest to compare some additional lines from Crashaw's poem immediately preceding those which Coleridge says he remembered as having suggested the theme of martyrdom as stated in the above passage. Crashaw says:

> *Love touched her heart, and, lo, it beats*
> *High, and burns with such brave heats,*
> *Such thirsts to die, as dares drink up*
> *A thousand cold deaths in one cup.*
> *Good reason; for she breathes all fire;*
> *Her white breast heaves with strong desire*
> *Of what she may, with fruitless wishes,*
> *Seek for amongst her mother's kisses.*

The imagery here suggests, or at least might have suggested to Coleridge, how intricately the desire for martyrdom is associated with the situation of the child nursing at the mother's breast. But one should remember too that while masochism and martyrdom have much in common, yet the theological implications of psychic masochism carry us beyond its psychological description.

The first part of *Christabel* was begun in 1797, but before it was finished Coleridge had started and completed *The Ancient Mariner*. The second part of *Christabel* was not begun until 1800. It will therefore be of interest to consider *The Ancient Mariner* before we look at the second part of *Christabel*. In this way we may be able to learn something about the progress Coleridge made in erecting defenses against his basic conflict.

The basic psychological situation to which Coleridge seems to be giving expression in *The Ancient Mariner* has its roots, as in *Christabel,* in the relation which the child has to its mother on the pregenital level of experience. It, like Christabel, is built around the masochistic fantasy which we have already pointed out as accounting for Coleridge's description of the horror of Geraldine's bosom. This unconscious fantasy of the phallic mother is one of the ways in which the child attempts to master its conflict with the mother's breast. It simply fantasies that it has a breast of its own, that is, an organ which dispenses liquid, in its own genitals. By means of this "autarchic fiction" it is enabled to reject the mother image as no longer needed since it now possesses a breast of its own. Unfortunately this defensive fantasy leads to serious trouble later in life when the individual may still be governed by unconscious rejection of the mother image and seek his (or her) sexual satisfaction only in a person of the same sex who possesses a "breast" like that of his own infantile fantasy. The possibilities for masochistic satisfaction are very great here for by means of the homosexual perversion the individual succeeds in frustrating his normal heterosexual tendencies. Such a person has never been able to overcome the unconscious infantile image of mother as a denier. Hence all of his (or her) actions are unconsciously motivated by the defensive desire to attack aggressively this mother image. Unfortunately the attacks are unconsciously fated to injure the individual himself more than any object external to him.

If, now, we turn to *The Ancient Mariner* we shall see how richly Coleridge has expressed this basic situation in symbolic terms. The fact that the poem is about a sailor makes it plausible that it should deal with homosexuality as one of its psychological themes, for sailors are traditionally afflicted with this perversion. The fact that the mariner is old may suggest that he has gone beyond the genital level of experience—just as the child at the breast has not yet reached it. Furthermore, as the poem opens we note that the mariner stops only one of the three wedding guests. This may be a hint at a belief common among homosexuals that they represent a third sex—the hermaphrodite or androgynous. The wedding guest himself, however, seems to have very strong heterosexual ties, for he is next of kin to the bridegroom.

But in spite of the contrasting allusion to the genital level of experience, the guest cannot escape the mariner. He manifests dread at the mariner's long gray beard and skinny hand, which may be regarded as phallic symbols, and he is particularly held by his glittering eye. Here we have the first allusion to the oral elements in the basic situation. For the eye is a passive organ which takes in what it sees just as the mouth takes in milk from the breast. The mariner therefore clings to the wedding guest as the child clings to the mother and the homosexual to his friend. The reversal of the roles in making the mariner (child) hold the wedding guest (mother) is the normal defense whereby an aggressive relation covers a basically passive one. This also appears in the fact that while the mariner's stare holds the listener (passive voyeurism and forcible restraint), his compulsive flow of words, unconsciously identified with milk, are an aggressive demonstration intended to refute the mother image. "I give, not you, bad mother." Almost immediately, however, there is a further reversal of the roles for the guest calls the mariner a "loon," thus identifying him with the giving yet, dreaded breast via the bird symbol, and the guest himself is called a three years child with whom the mariner is said to "have his will." The sexual overtones of this last phrase add to the sinister character of the mariner.

He now begins his story, relating how the ship leaves behind the kirk (perhaps a womb symbol, but at least a mother symbol), hill (breast), and lighthouse top (phallic breast), all three of which insofar as they represent his native country may indicate the widening rift between child and mother. The sun, which in classical mythology is Apollo, the archer god, and hence typical of the helpless infant who must aim its aggression at a distant object, is said to come up on the left and out of the sea. Like the mariner, he is fleeing the bad-mother image. For if we may take the sea as a mother symbol, as it often is in classical mythology (e.g., Thetis) due to its close associations with the moon goddess, then we can understand why the aggressive infant (sun, with a pun on son) leaves the sea on the sinister side, and why he returns to her on the right shining brightly. But as the sun climbs higher it comes to stand over the mast (phallus) at noon—and at this point the wedding guest breaks into the mariner's story in consternation, anticipating, perhaps, the homosexual symbolism of this juxtaposition of aggressive infant hovering over the phallic breast of the mother, that is, the mast of the ship. Significantly he beats his breast as he hears the bassoon (phallus) at the wedding festivities. He thinks of the bride coming into the hall "red as a rose." (This phrase may be an echo of Burns' lyric, "My love is like a red, red rose," in which the poet says he will love her until the sun dries up the seas and melts the rocks, which again suggests the enmity between the sun and mother on the pregenital level—if the rocks be taken as phallic symbols.) But the wedding guest cannot enjoy for long the comforting thoughts of the nodding heads of the minstrelsy, for the mariner forces his attention once more.

The ship is now caught by a storm whose overtaking wings suggests that the implacable breast has begun to persecute the masochistic infant in real earnest. Significantly we are now driven into the regions of intense cold where the warmth of love (as in the lowest circles of Dante's hell) is no longer available. The roaring suggests the child's projection of his own ravenous desires on the devouring mother image, the greenness of the ice his envy of the breast, the absence of men or beasts the abandoned aloneness of the infant. Finally the chief breast symbol, the albatross (a bird, but not a songbird and thus one that denies sounds-milk) appears, and the mariner, like the expectant infant, places all his hopes in it. The ice splits (perhaps a reminiscence of the birth trauma), and by a new reversal of the roles the albatross is said to eat the food it "ne'er had ate." The mariner is plainly doing his best to restrain his aggressive tendencies; the bird is complimented as a "Christian soul." It flies in circles to symbolize the circular shape of the breast, and it brings a south wind which suggests the climates of nudity and moral freedom. All the while, the moon, as grand archetypal mother symbol (Hecate, Lucina) glimmers through the mist, which, by some long leap of association, may allude to the most famous of mythological homosexuals, Achilles, whose name is associated with the Greek adjective for misty.

For nine vespers (suggestive of the nine-month-old child) the bird perches on the mast and then the mariner, with typical infantile unpredictability shoots it with his crossbow. We can now see another reason why the archer Apollo is to be identified with the pseudo-aggressive mariner. The crime has been committed, a crime whose violence reminds one of the pregenital violence of Achilles and Apollo in the *Iliad* and of Odysseus in the latter part of the *Odyssey*. The mariner moreover attacks the albatross under the light of the "white moonshine" of the mother symbol just as the child reacts aggressively to the frustrating breast.[6] The fact that in several previous instances of reversal of the roles the mariner has already appeared as identified with the breast (his compulsive speech, his being called a loon) suggests the masochistic, self-punishing aspect of the crime.

In the first lines of the second part we see that the sun now rises upon the right in leaving the sea and hence we suspect that it is now safer to flee the mother image than it was at first. Correspondingly when it goes into the sea, it goes shrouded in mist and on the left. The crime has made the difference. The sailors, feeling this clash between the sun and the sea symbols, accuse the mariner of gross ingratitude for his attack on the harmless breast-bird. But when the sun-mariner rises the next day, they suddenly change their opinion. Now they involve themselves in the guilt by saying that the mariner was right to kill the bird which brought the mist, though this obviously is untrue since the mist was there before the bird came. The sailors, it seems, are now willing to share the guilt because they think it is safe to do so—that is, because the sun is escaping the sea-mother. It is for this reason that they become accomplices in so unpromising a crime. The ship, however, enters a silent sea and thus the blame is once more laid on the denying-mother symbol via the identification of words and milk. The white foam flies, but the furrow is always being left behind. Now, too, the motive power of the ship, which may symbolize the attraction between the sexes in heterosexual relations, is lost. The sails, as breast symbols, drop down and the men speak only to break the silence of the sea, that is, to refute the image of the denying mother.

Still more ominously, the sun, in its cheap ("copper" money) sky, is bloody to signify the cannibalistic desires of the nursing infant, and at noon, for a second time, stands above the mast no bigger than the moon—again an attempt to shift the blame to the mother symbol. The homosexual lack of real creativity is once more stressed in the failure of the ship to move, but the blame is further shifted to the mother in the image of the painted ship and ocean which suggest the painted woman as harlot. The punishing thirst of the aggressive babe desiring the breast now asserts itself with intolerable insistence. The boards of the ship-mother shrink and the sea rots. The suggestion of moral perversion in this last calls forth the imprecation: "O Christ, that ever this should be!" Now, too, the sea begins to crawl with slimy water snakes, symbols of the breast-phallus which motivates the homosexual relationship. The death fires, will-o'-the-wisps which lead men astray into the marshes of the feminine genitals, dance about the ship, and the water is witch's oil. The allusion to the witches in *Macbeth* points up the bad-mother symbolism. Further, a spirit, nine fathoms deep, now dogs the ship, and the sailors, under the spell of the breast complex, take the mariner for a mother image and attach themselves to him with their evil looks. Finally to stress the masochistic nature of the homosexual rejection of the mother, the slaughtered breast-albatross is hung about the mariner's neck instead of the cross. There is also a hidden defense involved in this symbolic act, for it may mean: "I am not aggressive against the breast, I hug it to me." But the important point is that the nature of the mariner's punishment, that is, self-punishment, has been made clear. He must give, as a mother, sights-milk to those evil eyes-mouths of the men who hate him; he must suffer from a thirst which was presumably the motive for his infantile aggression; and he must identify himself with the breast which he has attacked and will continue to attack by hanging it around his neck. Thus the object of his aggression always turns out to be himself.

Part three contains the first defense against this masochistic conflict with the mother. It is not, however, the homosexual fantasy which has only been obscurely hinted at in part two and which will not be fully developed until part four, but something quite different. There are some indications that the blame for inordinate thirst is being placed where it belongs in the image of the man choked with soot and the glazing of the eyes: the organs receptive of sight-nourishment. But a mother image which will prove an adequate scapegoat soon appears in the form of the phantom ship. The mariner has to bite his arm for blood, a sort of cannibal vampirism, in order to proclaim what everyone can see for himself, namely, the approach of a sail-breast symbol. The crew grin with ghastly irony and significantly draw in their breath as if drinking. The grin, as Professor Lowes has pointed out, was probably associated in Coleridge's mind with thirst he experienced while climbing Paenman Mawr mountain—again a breast symbol. But this ship, too, has no normal heterosexual motive power, for she moves without a breeze. As she moves between the mariner and the sun it seems as if she is a skeleton through whose ribs the sun peers as through the grate of a dungeon. There are appeals for grace to the mother of heaven, and there is perhaps a pun on "goosemere" (French gosse, boy; mere, mother) which describes the sails. It now becomes apparent that we have a fantasy of the child imprisoned in the womb. The woman Life-in-Death is the mother who denies life to the child she carries within her.

> *Are those* her *ribs through which the Sun*
> *Did peer, as through a grate?*
> *And is that Woman all her crew?*
> *Is that a DEATH? and are there two?*
> *Is DEATH that woman's mate?*

The collocation of a woman and a skeleton is a well-known medieval inconograph used to illustrate the danger of feminine wiles—but perhaps its ultimate meaning is that the denying mother reduces her son to a starved skeleton. And there are other touches to suggest the lack of real love and untouchability of the prostitute.

> Her *lips were red,* her *looks were free,*
> *Her locks were yellow as gold:*
> *Her skin was as white as leprosy,*
> *The Night-mare LIFE-IN-DEATH was she,*
> *Who thicks man's blood with cold.*

She plays at dice, a masochistically tinged game of chance, and wins the mariner from her shipmate death, though this is small consolation for him since she whistles thrice and thus suggests that masochistic homosexuality which as third sex is a fate worse than death.

But she disappears when the moon comes out to take her place; the horned moon, now the phallic mother, with a star within its nether tip like an infant at the breast-phallus. (One might also recall Homer's comparison of Achilles to the dog star, and the dogs which attend on Hecate.) Fear drinks the mariner's life blood as at a cup. The crew fall down dead, punished for no other crime than having halfheartedly approved of the mariner's act. They are to serve as homosexual mother images for the mariner and hence they must be dead so that he may have his masochistic attachment to Life-in-Death. But the main burden of part three has been the attempt to shift the blame on the mother image by making her the jailer of the child in the womb. The refrain would run: "How can I be aggressive against the breast when mother imprisons me and denies me life?" This is the first defense, and not wholly successful; for the section ends with the souls of the crew departing like the whizz of the crossbow, thus recalling the original crime. Indeed, the image of the child as prisoner in the womb, already suggests that it is at least a suspected criminal.

In part four we have expression of the second and major defense, that of the homosexual fantasy. Significantly again it begins with a fearful interruption on the part of the wedding guest. But the mariner reassures him and stresses the pitiful plight of the infant alone and abandoned on the wide sea. This implied reproach against the mother image is followed by further homosexual aggression.

> *The many men, so beautiful!*
> *And they all dead did lie:*
> *And a thousand thousand slimy things*
> *Lived on; and so did I.*

One might suppose that this exclamation is really more expressive of necrophilia than homosexuality; however, it presently appears that the men are not altogether dead. They are reanimated in order to navigate the ship. One might almost say that they are dead to heterosexual attachments, but alive to homosexual ones. Still the mariner tries to pray, but the identification with the denying mother prevents this. He closes his lids and his eyes beat like pulses-lips at the breast, while sea and sky lie like a load upon the eyes and the dead are at his feet. They continue to look at him and this he finds more horrible than an orphan's curse which drags a spirit from on high. The gloss at this point is interesting, for it tells how the mariner yearns towards the moon. The stars-mariners, too, find that the sky belongs to them, is their appointed, native country, and natural home where they are expected with silent joy. The other side of this attempt at reassuring defense is given in the verses where the moon is said to be unstable and that it mocks the sultry main with its cold hoarfrost. The ambivalence toward the mother image is plain.

But the charmed water of the sea-mother now assumes a bloody appearance and the water snakes rear and shake off their elfish light in hoary flakes. Their richness is irresistibly attractive to the mariner, and as he views them in relation to the light of the bad moon-mother he feels a spring of love gush from his heart.

> O happy living things! no tongue
> Their beauty might declare:
> A spring of love gushed from my heart,
> And I blessed them unaware:
> Sure my kind saint took pity on me,
> And I blessed them unaware.

But all this is really only a defense against the masochistic subjection to the mother, for the mariner now seems to say that he accepts the breast in its phallic form, though in doing so he rejects the mother in her truly feminine role. That he is deceiving himself seems even more likely when we are twice told that he blesses the snakes unawares—i.e., without the sanction of reason and consciousness. And since he has now accepted the breast-phallus as no longer reprehensible, the symbol of the masochistic attachment to the breast per se, the albatross, can be dispensed with and it accordingly drops from his neck back to the sea where it belongs—i.e., to the mother. This second defense, then, far from meaning any sort of ultimate salvation for the mariner, only rivets his masochistic attachment to the mother image more firmly. He makes a fatal mistake in blessing the water snakes, for this means that he ceases to fight against the homosexual fantasy.

There is some realization of the gravity of the mariner's situation in the fifth part, for here a third defense is raised, again quite different from the preceding two. The Mother of Christ now sends the mariner sleep during which he dreams that the buckets on the deck are filled with dew—an attempt to nullify his fantasy of the denying mother. But though he awakens and though it rains, he still seems to be in a trance during which he witnesses a storm—a strangely unreal one for it never comes near the ship and thus has no validity for the mariner's case. This storm seems to be a heterosexual coitus fantasy. The aurora borealis is seen to move to and fro while the wan stars dance in between. There is perhaps a suggestion of the feminine genitals in the sighing sedge, the one black cloud from which the rain pours, and the moon at its edge. And the cloud is cleft, and the lightning, perhaps an allusion to the highly potent Zeus, falls in between. But the whole defense is further proved unreal by the fact that the ship begins to move in its unnatural way again. The dead men become erect and their actions are sanctioned by being said to be due to blessed spirits. Thus the homosexual defense once more takes precedence. The mariner and the body of his brother's son stand knee to knee pulling at the same rope. (Here again, it is noteworthy, the wedding guest fearfully interrupts, for he sees the homosexual allusion.) But when dawn comes the dead crew clusters around the mast-phallus and sounds-milk fly up to the sun. This homosexual attempt to simulate the giving breast is symbolized to the mariner first by his hearing the skylark, bird-breast, then by his comparison of it to a lonely flute-phallus, then to an angel's song (angels are hermaphrodite) that makes heaven mute. When they cease the sails continue the sounds until noon, like a brook on a June night—perhaps the height of ambivalent indecision!

At noon, when the sun is over the mast again, the ship ceases to be moved by the homosexual spirit from beneath. Then it begins to move again with a backward-and-forward motion, like a pawing horse, a common feminine symbol, and the mariner's blood is flung to his head. The heterosexual coitus defense has thus been momentarily and violently reasserted. But it breaks down almost immediately, for when the mariner awakens out of his fit he hears two spirits discussing his pregenital, masochistic crime in the plainest terms. The gloss tells us that penance long and heavy for the mariner has been accorded to the polar spirit. Evidently the homosexual defense involved in blessing the water snakes has been of no avail either. The homosexual fantasy, now seemingly personified in the polar spirit, demands its own punishment in conformity with its masochistic origin. There is also irony in the way the albatross is spoken of in the male gender by the two spirits.

In the sixth part the mariner begins to make some progress toward stabilization of the conflict. A summary may be of value here. Up to this time the poem has been occupied with the various defenses which are thrown up to disguise the real nature of the masochistic conflict and escape the guilt which attaches to the passivity which lies at its root. This basic passivity may be expressed in terms of the sentence: "I *want* Mother to abandon, reject, and punish me." The reaction to this state of mind is an aggressive defense, symbolized by the shooting of the albatross. The guilt of having submitted too far is thus alleviated, only to accept another burden of guilt for having attacked too strongly. The other defenses which then appear are further attempts to escape the problem of an objective estimate of the child's relation to the mother—neither too passive nor too aggressive. The defense involved in the phantom bark scene is an attempt to put the blame for the child's passivity on the mother image by regressing even more deeply than the pregenital level, that is, to the period when the child is in the womb. The defenses involved in the various coitus symbols of the storm and rocking ship are attempts to escape the pregenital conflict by focusing attention on the genital level of experience. The homosexual defense, however, is built on the pregenital level, but it escapes the guilt of extreme passivity and aggression against the mother image by simply rejecting her entire sex! There is of course a good deal of aggression hidden within this defense and in order to overcome this it must be sublimated.

It is for this reason that part six involves such a sublimation of the homosexual defense. It opens with the conversation of the two voices—indications that the mariner is achieving a certain amount of objectivity with regard to his crime. One of these explains that the ocean only moves the ship insofar as it is a slave of the moon who is gracious. This is perhaps an attempt to reconcile the ambivalent aspects of the mother image. We also learn that the ship is moving faster than human life can endure, perhaps another indication of the perverted, aggressive character of the mariner who is still in a trance. When he awakens, the gloss tells us that his penance is to begin anew. The moon is high, the dead men stand together in homosexual solidarity. The charnel dungeon atmosphere suggests Juliet insane in the potion scene, and the men's stony eyes recall the dreadful-mother image of the Medusa. But the curse which is in their eyes (not the curse which attaches to the mariner's crime of killing the albatross) is suddenly snapped. The mariner is relieved but still pursued by some frightful fiend—i.e., the mother *(cf.* Coleridge's poem "Love" and the offerings given to Hecate by throwing them over the shoulder without looking backward). The ship begins to move in an uncanny fashion. The breeze blows upon the mariner but not upon the sea-mother. It mingles strangely with his fears, and yet it brings him joyfully to his home harbor. The mariner is evidently still in his homosexual trance, though he prays to be relieved of it. But the peculiar ambivalence of the mother image appears in the ominous mention of the shadow of the moon and the silentness of the moonlight.

The new and sublimated defense now begins to be evident. For from the corpses of the dead, which now lie flat to indicate that all the sensual homosexual tendencies have been driven out, there arise crimson shadows in the shape of seraph-men. We remember that Milton's angels are hermaphrodites and even though they only inhabit *Paradise Lost* they are still wonderful sublimations of .the homosexual fantasy. But they inspire horror too, and the cross is invoked. Still the mariner seems more content with this defence than with any of the preceding ones. The seraphs are a heavenly, lovely sight to him and even their silence sinks like music in his soul. They have, moreover, lured the pilot and his boy, mother and son, to the ship. Still torn by ambivalence, the mariner says that not even the seraphs can blast the joy he feels at the approach of these two, thus suggesting how deeply he dreads the seraphs. But he also hears the hermit who is an even better sublimation of homosexual, masochistic tendencies than the seraph-men. It is the hermit who brings with him the sanction of religious tradition for asceticism-masochism and solitude (homosexuality in the sense that female society is rejected) that will, the mariner thinks, wash away the blood of the breast complex.

The seventh and last part of the poem contains the final statement of the sublimation which the mariner has achieved. The hermit evidently plays a very large part in it. We are told that he sings sweetly and thus has a more stable defense against the denying-mother image than the seraph-men who were silent. He loves to talk with sailors, which suggests that he has sublimated homosexual tendencies, the rotted oak and stump-phallus breast on which he prays is wholly hidden by moss. Moreover, he understands what the mariner has been through, for he says that the sails of the ship are like skeletons of leaves that lay along the forest brook—i.e., like babes starving at the breast, when the owl (Athena as aggressive mother image) calls to the wolf that devours the she-wolf's offspring. The pilot, however, has none of the cheery confidence which the hermit has, and when their boat approaches the ship there is a violent explosion which splits the bay and sinks the ship down in a whirlpool—Charybdis and the feminine genitals! This, perhaps, is a last attempt to shift the blame for the mariner's defensive aggression to the mother image by means of a violent birth fantasy. But such a crude defense is again totally unsuccessful. For the pilot, in whose boat the mariner neatly lands, realizes that he is guilty of dreadful crimes and consequently falls down in a fit. The pilot's boy, too, fearing the mariner's homosexuality and the dreadful mother image he bears within him, immediately goes crazy and makes a grim joke about the mariner's facility with the oar-phallus.

Even the hermit finds it pretty hard to take the mariner as he is, and hence can scarcely stand when he goes out of the boat. In answer to the mariner's request that he be shriven, the hermit asks what manner of man he is. The mariner does not reply, but is forced to tell his story. This compulsory giving of words-milk is intended to refute the denying-mother image, as Christabel's silence is a similar aggressive refutation. We see that the mariner has not conquered his basic conflict, for this compulsory giving is a recurrent symptom; at the same time we get an insight into the mechanism which makes the "born writer" productive of such quantities of words. (Here we may also see a further connection between Apollo, the mariner, and Coleridge himself. For Apollo was the slayer of the Python-phallic breast which is buried under the omphalos where the Delphic oracles are given and where the priestess gives forth her mantic sayings. It is thus understandable why this god with an oral complex should become the god of poetry.) It is also understandable why Coleridge should bring the mariner around to this sort of punishment which is not only a punishment for himself but also an attack on the mother image. Unfortunately for him, the writer's block which he expressed so poignantly in *Christabel* made writing more of a punishment than it is for most poets. And while in Coleridge's case the compulsive giving, or not giving, of words was not associated with overt homosexuality, it was true, as he probably knew, of Sophocles and, as he could suspect, of Shakespeare and many other writers.

In any event the mariner now says that he passes like night, that is, under the influence of the moon-mother image, from land to land, and that he always knows the particular sort of man who must hear him, that is, we suspect, the homosexual. Significantly, the unwelcome sounds of the wedding come to his ears as an uproar, but the monastic sound of the vesper bell soothes him with the thought of the ascetic discipline of prayer. He hastens to explain to the wedding guest that this preference is due to the fact that he has been abandoned on the wide sea-mother. And then he exclaims:

O sweeter than the marriage-feast,
'Tis sweeter far to me,
To walk together to the kirk
With a goodly company!—

This stanza explicitly states the sublimation whereby the homosexual asceticism of religion (the walk to the church as sublimated mother image) is placed on a higher level than the more normal attitude of heterosexuality. It explains the mariner's contention that:

He prayeth best, who loveth best
All things both great and small;
For the dear God who loveth us,
He made and loveth all.

The all-inclusive nature of this social ideal of unity, it seems, has its roots in homosexual ties. It appears to be a fact that the great socializing institutions such as monasticism in the Middle Ages, political parties, educational institutions, clubs, and secret societies today have usually functioned most efficiently when segregation of the sexes has been enforced and when homosexual ties, in a sublimated form, were at their strongest.[7] On the other hand, the family, which is based on heterosexual ties, seems to have certain antisocial characteristics which tend to split the mass into atomic groups. It is for this reason that the mariner succeeds in getting the wedding guest to turn from the bridegroom's door, and it is for this reason that old men, babes, loving friends, youths and maidens gay must bend to the great Father who is not a father in any real sense but only in the sublimated sense that he blends all humanity into one group. The use of the heterosexual term, father, here shows how flexible the sublimation of homosexual traits can be.

. . . and now the Wedding-Guest
Turned from the bridegroom's door.

He went like one that hath been stunned,
And is of sense forlorn:
A sadder and a wiser man,
He rose the morrow morn.

In order to avoid misunderstanding of this interpretation of *The Ancient Mariner*, it should again be stressed that Coleridge is not here giving direct expression to his own homosexual traits. There is no biographical evidence that he had overt homosexual tendencies, although his intimate friendships with Lamb, Southey, and Wordsworth are relevant clues as to the importance of the fantasy to him. It was in collaboration with the latter friend that this poem was begun, though they soon parted company over it; and Coleridge's first meeting with the Wordsworths was at a time when he was having marital difficulties, one of which was that "dear Sara," his wife, spilled a pan of boiling milk on his foot which prevented him taking walks with his new friends for several days! But the important point, as previously stressed, is that Coleridge is using his attitude toward homosexuality in this poem as a defense against the still more basic conflict of psychic masochism insofar as it relates to the unconscious mother image. He is, so to speak, solving the problem temporarily by accepting the guilt for the lesser crime, hoping that this alibi will carry him through. It did not, for we know that his masochistic tendencies never left him, but the attempt was remarkable nevertheless.

We may now return to the second part of *Christabel*. It is to some extent a new poem, none too well integrated with the first part, though there is much in it which lends support to the interpretation given up to this point. Such, for example, is Christabel's feeling that she has sinnned as she awakens in the morning and watches Geraldine's heaving breasts. Such, too, is her prayer to the suffering Christ to wash away those sins. But the most difficult problem which it poses is the relationship which now develops between Christabel and her father. From one point of view it is what we should expect since if the basic theme of the poem relates to the masochistic relationship between mother and child, then there should be a corresponding devotion between father and child to serve as a defense against it. But this attachment to the father and the consequent struggle to warn him of the evil power of Geraldine is really not the most puzzling aspect of the second part. It could be explained on the ground that Geraldine has already manifested herself as an evil influence to Christabel and hence it is only natural that the latter wishes to save her father from the witch. What is puzzling is the father's suddenly developed anger against Christabel. There seems to be no reason for this in view of the fact that Coleridge has already stressed the deep bond which exists between them. Some light may be thrown upon the problem, however, if we again assume that Coleridge and Christabel have the same unconscious identity. We then have a father-son relationship along the lines of the negative oedipus pattern which involves a feminine identification. For here again we have to do with a defense against the reproach that Coleridge is guilty of psychic masochism due to the mother-son relationship. The new defense runs: "No, it is not true that I am masochistically attached to mother. I love her and for this reason father hates me."

One or two matters which substantiate this view may be noted. First, Coleridge's characterization of Sir Leoline suggests that he is building an oedipal pattern into the plot which can be used as a defense against the oral masochistic pattern. For the chief reason that Sir Leoline accepts Geraldine with so much affectionate display is that he discovers her to be the daughter of his onetime friend, Sir Roland de Vaux. Now the passage in which Sir Leoline laments this ancient break is said by E. H. Coleridge to refer to Coleridge's friendship with Southey (other editors say Lamb). The image which is used to describe this break is curious.

> *They stood aloof, the scars remaining,*
> *Like cliffs which had been rent asunder;*
> *A dreary sea now flows between;—*
> *But neither heat, nor frost, nor thunder,*
> *Shall wholly do away, I ween,*
> *The marks of that which once hath been.*

The cliffs may refer to the two friends, but then what is the intervening sea? May the figure not also be read as a coitus symbol as G. Wilson Knight has suggested in commenting on the line in *Kubla Khan* about the sacred river Alph? It would seem plausible if this passage is an allusion to Coleridge's break with Southey. For about the same time as this break occurred, Coleridge gained his wife Sara, and not long thereafter their son Hartley was born. The fact that Coleridge refers to, or is said to refer to, his young son Hartley in the conclusion to Part II, seems also to fit in with these conjectures. Further, the fact that Coleridge terms the break between the friends "a dreary sea" may be an echo of the unhappiness of his relations with Sara, and the reunion of Sir Leoline and Sir Roland may be an attempt to patch up the strained relations which existed between Coleridge, his wife, and his friends. But such a change in affairs, that is, love between Geraldine and Sir Leoline, could only work to estrange Sir Leoline from Christabel, and this new rift between father and child is a distraction from the defense against the old rift between mother and child. In any case it seems clear that Geraldine alone is capable of making Sir Leoline forget that 'world of death" which was his ever since the death of his first wife and the loss of his friend —all of which makes him so ominous to poor Christabel at the beginning of the second part of the poem. It is true that Geraldine is not specifically designated as Sir Leoline's wife-to-be, but she has plainly displaced Christabel in his affections. Consequently the hatred which Sir Leoline shows for Christabel may be taken as a manifestation of the oedipus pattern—even though Christabel, for her part, protests that she loves her father. This love, indeed, may be a trace of the negative oedipus complex wherein the feminine identification is typical, and would account for Coleridge's choice of a female protagonist.

We may further note several interesting points in connection with the dream which Bard Bracy tells in order to deter Sir Leoline in his plan to aid Geraldine. It is curious that the snake which figures in it is one which strangles, not stings, its victim. Bard Bracy says:

> . . . I saw a bright green snake
> Coiled around its wings and neck.
> Green as the herbs on which it couched,
> Close by the dove's its head it crouched
> And with the dove it heaves and stirs,
> Swelling its neck as she swelled hers!

Seeing that the snake is not a boa constrictor, and hence not one of the ordinary strangling variety, this suggests the typical oral symptom of choking or gagging as a defense against oral desires. But the important point is that while Bard Bracy equates Geraldine to the snake and Christabel to the dove, Sir Leoline does not. He looks upon the snake as Geraldine's enemies and the dove as Geraldine. (Compare the ambivalent nature of the albatross in *The Ancient Mariner* as a bird of good and bad omen.) This leads us to suspect that unconsciously Coleridge is again reversing the roles and making Geraldine into the innocent and Christabel into the evil aggressor. The suspicion is perhaps confirmed in the passage where Geraldine transfers to Christabel her snakelike characteristics.

> So deeply had she drunken in
> That look, those shrunken serpent eyes,
> That all her features were resigned
> To this sole image in her mind;
> And passively did imitate
> That look of dull and treacherous hate!
> And thus she stood, in dizzy trance,
> Still picturing that look askance
> With forced unconscious sympathy
> Full before her father's view—

There is a further suggestion of the oedipal pattern in the last lines of the poem where Coleridge describes Sir Leoline's wrath against Christabel.

The dishonor she has brought him by warning him (appealing as she does so to her mother's soul) against "the wronged daughter of a friend" is said to be due to "more than woman's jealousy." This cryptic phrase may allude to the underlying identification between Coleridge and Christabel and the new orientation which he wished to give it along oedipal lines. We may in this connection note that a possible source for this Lamia-like character of Geraldine, and consequently of Christabel, is Burton's account of the Lamia which in turn is drawn from Mizaldus' story of Alexander the Great's encounter with the poisonous Indian serpent maiden. This source is valuable because here, for the first time, we see the bad mother-child relationship hinted at in terms of the mother-son relationship, as opposed to that of mother-daughter. But in the end, the guilt lies with Christabel, and Coleridge's attempt to build a convincing oedipal pattern breaks down precisely because the more fundamental oral pattern is inescapable. Always she must face the horror of her aggression and passivity.

> *Again she saw that bosom old,*
> *Again she felt that bosom cold,*
> *And drew in her breath with a hissing sound;*

Even on the oedipal level Coleridge only succeeds in placing the guilt where it does not belong, namely: on Christabel's defenses against passivity. She becomes the aggressor not only against the bad-mother image, Geraldine, but also against her father, in taking on Geraldine's malicious characteristics. And yet she cannot help showing the most passionate love, in negative oedipal fashion, for that same father, and an equally strong attachment for the bad mother. The plot has arrived at an inextricable impasse. The repeated assertions of Christabel's innocence only serve to point up the fact that somehow she is terribly and hopelessly in the wrong. It is now more clear than ever why Geraldine is in this part too sometimes described as not wanting to harm Christabel and even dreading her. And we can perhaps understand, too, why the poem was never finished.

The conclusion to Part II, which has been supposed to be an irrelevant fragment for the poet's son, Hartley Coleridge, is now seen to make sense with the main psychological theme of the poem. The lines are a richly significant description of infantile feelings of self-sufficiency and omnipotence which, having been injured by fancied parental neglect, proceed to provoke a punitive attitude in the parents—once again the infantile tendency to turn its own aggressive against itself.

> *A little child, a limber elf,*
> *Singing, dancing to itself,*
> *A fairy thing with red round cheeks,*
> *That always finds, and never seeks,*
> *Makes such a vision to the sight*
> *As fills a father's eyes with light;*
> *And pleasures flow in so thick and fast*
> *Upon his heart, that he at last*
> *Must needs express his love's excess*
> *With words of unmeant bitterness.*

Coleridge's comment on these lines that they are a "very metaphysical account of fathers' calling their children rogues, rascals, and little varlets" bears out this supposition that the passage has an essential relation to the theme of psychic masochism—though here again the roles of persecutor and persecuted, in accord with the negative oedipus fantasy, are reversed. The same point is made when Coleridge says that:

> *Perhaps 'tis pretty to force together*
> *Thoughts so all unlike each other;*
> *To mutter and mock a broken charm,*
> *To dally with wrong that does no harm.*
> *Perhaps 'tis tender too and pretty*
> *At each wild word to feel within*
> *A sweet recoil of love and pity.*

That is to say, the defensive aggression with which the psychic masochist unconsciously provokes his daily dose of pain is the only means he has of obtaining the love and pity which more normal people obtain in less self-damaging ways. The psychic masochist must "mutter and mock a broken charm," the mother image, and "dally with wrong that does no harm"—consciously. The words with which Coleridge concludes the poem have a deep and poignant meaning.

> *. . . what if in a world of sin*
> *(O sorrow and shame should this be true!)*
> *Such giddiness of heart and brain*
> *Comes seldom save from rage and pain*
> *So talks as it's most used to do.*

What, then, are we led to conclude as to the value of this reading of the psychological theme of the poem? We can see first of all that the surface inconsistencies with which it is burdened diminish when we take into account

Coleridge's unconscious psychological presuppositions. The apparently un-motivated dread which Geraldine inspires in Christabel, the attraction which Christabel nevertheless has to Geraldine, and the hatred which Sir Leoline develops for Christabel make sense. We can see, too, why the poem exercises such a powerful, yet inexplicable, fascination upon the minds of its readers. It is, among other reasons, because Coleridge has delved so deeply into the unconscious sources of an important human trait which is to some extent characteristic of everyone, namely: psychic masochism, that it continues to exert its magic effect. Coleridge was of course not the only Romantic poet to concern himself with this trait. As we shall see they were all much concerned with it, and among the prose writers, De Quincey, in his essay entitled "Levana and our Lady of Sorrows," shows real insight into it. They were all preoccupied with the secularized version of what in the Middle Ages was sanctioned as asceticism and in classical times shrouded by the mystery cults. It is true that the many disguises and defenses which we have discovered in the poem show us that Coleridge cannot face the central problem directly. But this does not in any way detract from the communicative power of the poem. On the contrary it adds to its value for Coleridge's readers are just as much in need of these defenses against this inner peril as he was himself.

There is a good deal of evidence from Coleridge's biography that he had strong psychic masochistic tendencies which can be, as we have seen, traced to situations which center around the breast complex. He was a member of a large family in which there were already four girls and eight boys before he, the last of these, was born in 1772. In a letter to Sir George Beaumont in 1804 he wrote: "I was hardly used from infancy to boyhood, and from boyhood to youth most, *most* cruelly." It was the nurse of his handsome brother Francis who tormented him as a child, though we should remember that it is Coleridge's subjective reactions which are given in the above quotation. But even though this old nurse was to some extent a "bad mother" to him, his relationship to his real mother was not always amiable either. An anecdote given in Coleridge's own words in a letter to Thomas Poole, dated 16 October 1797, shows some of the traits of orally determined masochism.

I had asked my mother one evening to cut my cheese entire, so that I might toast it. This was no easy matter, it being a *crumbly* cheese. My mother, however, did it. I went into the garden for something or other, and in the mean time my brother Frank *minced* my cheese "to disappoint the favorite." I returned, saw the exploit, and in an agony of passion flew at Frank. He pretended to have been seriously hurt by my blow, flung himself on the ground, and there lay with outstretched limbs. I hung over him moaning, and in a great fright; he leaped up, and with a horse-laugh gave me a severe blow in the face. I seized a knife, and was running at him, when my mother came in and took me by the arm. I expected a flogging, and struggling from her I ran away to a hill at the bottom of which the Otter flows, about one mile from Ottery. There I stayed; my rage died away, but my obstinacy vanquished my fears, and taking out a little shilling book which had, at the end, morning and evening prayers, I very devoutly repeated them—thinking at the *same time* with inward and gloomy satisfaction how miserable my mother must be! . . .

Coleridge spent the night in the fields and was so stiff and cold and terrified by morning that he could not move from the bank of the flooded Otter. The following day he was found by a searching party. The effect of this incident turns up in later life when Coleridge makes the decision to go to London from Bristol. In a letter explaining his decision he makes the following curious slip: "I love Bristol and I do not love London—But there are two Giants leagued together, whose most imperious commands I must obey, however reluctant—their names are BREAD and CHEESE." The change from "bread and butter" to "bread and cheese" may indicate how a trivial conflict over food lingered in Coleridge's mind, and may point to the deeper oral motivation of his psychic masochism. It is also true that Coleridge ascribed the beginning of his ague, which later forced him to the opium habit, to this incident. (The symbols of the "horse-laugh," the hill, and the flooded river, all suggestive of the giving mother, should not be overlooked.) It seems clear in this anecdote that Coleridge feels that he was a terribly mistreated child; but it is also clear that in some way he enjoyed being mistreated.

Kenneth Burke has suggested another instance which, it seems to me, may be interpreted as further evidence of Coleridge's oral traits. He puts the unhappy marital relations of Coleridge with his wife Sara into the context of a choice between succumbing to the oral craving for opium and the responsibility to support Sara and her child. On the basis of our theory the choice would have been an important one for Coleridge. Coleridge thought the drug habit-forming, and he was thus provided with a convenient masochistic alibi for satisfying his unconscious oral desires (by taking opium) and at the same time refusing the support which his wife could reasonably claim from him. And this he could do on the grounds that the opium habit rendered him incapable of supporting her. He could thus play the denier

with good conscience and at the same time satisfy his masochistic tendencies by provoking the reproaches of society and his wife for failure to perform his ordinary duties. The devious shifts here ascribed to Coleridge may
at first seem unlikely, but the repetition of an infantile conflict with the bad
mother seems unmistakable.

Coleridge's biographer, Lawrence Hanson, remarks on his "perfect
genius" for making bad impressions, and this trait may very well have been
motivated by unconscious psychic masochism which constantly forced him
to put himself in the wrong with other people. The tendency toward self-
abasement is also a part of the masochistic substructure. A passage from a
letter written by Coleridge to explain the delay in the publication of *Christabel* affords an interesting example of this.

The delay in copy has been owing in part to me, as the writer of "Christabel." Every line has been produced by me with labor pangs. I abandon
poetry altogether— I leave the higher and deeper kinds to Wordsworth, the
delightful, popular and simply dignified to Southey; and reserve for myself
the honorable attempt to make others feel and understand their writings, as
they deserve to be felt and understood.

The difficulties which Coleridge experienced in writing poetry were of course
real enough, but the setting up of Wordsworth and Southey as superior
poets was hardly borne out by contemporary opinion and certainly is not
by present-day judgment.

The whole problem of the relation of the taking of opium to the composition of Coleridge's four major poems must, I think, also be noted in
connection with the hypothesis of Coleridge's orally determined masochism.
For the composition of the poems is precisely such a defense against the
reproaches of the inner conscience as we should expect under the circumstances. When conscience reproached him with inhibiting his artistic production with the opium habit the poems were there as an obvious refutation. Unfortunately there were only fragments for the most part, though
in Coleridge's imagination there were whole volumes. And when conscience
attacked not only the oral character of the habit but also its masochistic
character, he could say, in the case of *Christabel* at least, it is not I who am
masochistic, it is Christabel. In this connection Coleridge's account of the
composition of the second part of the poem is worth noting.

Immediately on my arrival in this country [after his return from Germany]
I undertook to finish a poem which I had begun, entitled "Christabel," for
a second volume of the *Lyrical Ballads*. I tried to perform my promise; but
the deep unutterable disgust, which I had suffered in the translations of that

accursed Wallenstein, seemed to have stricken me with barrenness, and nothing would come of it. I desisted with a deeper dejection than I am willing to remember. The wind from Skiddaw and Borrowdale was often as loud as wind need be—and many a walk in the clouds on the mountains did I take: but all would not do—till one day I dined out at the house of a neighboring clergyman, and somehow or other drank so much wine, that I found myself on the hither edge of sobriety. The next day my verse making faculties returned to me, and I proceeded successfully—till my poem grew so long and in Wordsworth's opinion so impressive, that he rejected it from his volume as disportionate both in size and merit and as discordant in its character.

It is interesting to speculate on the unconscious argument involved here. Psychiatric research has shown that drunkards often try to refute the mother image by identifying with it and "poisoning" themselves with liquor in order to show, masochistically, that mother is a poisoner. Perhaps Coleridge's writing block with respect to *Christabel* may be viewed as a defense against this sort of psychic masochism. On the basis of the identification between words and liquid nourishment this defense says: "No, it is not mother who has denied me, it is I who deny her." But the shock which Coleridge's potation at the clergyman's house administered to his unconscious balance may have been just enough to force him to drop, momentarily, the defense involved in his writing block. He could no longer say that mother denied him, and therefore that he must deny her in turn. But he could say she denied him good nourishment. Here again conscience attacked him and forced him to substitute another defense calculated to refute the reproach that he made the fantasied bad mother into a poisoner. This time it was: "No, it is not I-mother who poison myself; on the contrary I give words to others." The second part of *Christabel* was perhaps the result.

The supposition, then, that Coleridge was himself plagued by the same oral-masochistic conflict with the parents which we have hinted at in *Christabel* and *The Ancient Mariner* seems to have some basis in biographical evidence. No attempt has of course been made to typify Coleridge's character once and for all with this single trait. These incidents do, however, strengthen the likelihood that the poems could have been composed as defenses against those self-damaging tendencies which seem to have been a constant source of pain to Coleridge.

III

WORDSWORTH

Lines Composed a Few Miles Above Tintern Abbey
Ode: Intimations of Immortality • *Michael* • *Laodamia*

WORDSWORTH'S poetry shows us quite a different aspect of the unconscious conflict with the pregenital mother image. Whereas in Coleridge we see the conflict expressed in such a way that all the terms are adequately represented, this is not the case in Wordsworth. A hasty reader of some of Wordsworth's more famous poems might gain the impression that he suffered from no inner conflicts. A glance at his biography would dispell this impression. His early years, for example, were far from calm and happy. The restlessness and turbulence of his troubled soul is certainly expressed in the revolutionary attitude toward his native country and in espousing the cause of the French republic. There is also the affair with Annette Vallon and the subsequent repudiation of France and acceptance of conservatism. Many of these biographical facts (to be considered more fully later) suggest that Wordsworth was expressing his aggression against the mother image, as symbolized by the mother country, Annette Vallon, and France, in action rather than in poetry. The poetry, in fact, seems to be an attempt to deny the aggression which is so conspicuous in his actions. If this is so, we may find his poetry to be an expression of what is known as a magic gesture.

A magic gesture is the end result of an unconscious conflict whereby the individual dramatizes in his own behavior and character a formula which in its positive aspect says: "I will show you, bad mother, how I wanted to be treated," and in its negative form: "I will show you how I did not want to be treated." This attitude, however, already implies a deeper masochistic substratum which has been primarily warded off with defensive aggression. The aggression was in turn forbidden by the unconscious conscience and the attitudes of the magic gesture are then produced as acceptable substitutes which will serve as adequate defenses against the basic passivity.[1] The magic gestures does not indicate any conscious insincerity on the part of the individual who expresses it, but to an observer it will seem as if the individual displays striking inconsistencies in his character which he is nevertheless unable to reconcile. In Wordsworth's case, for example, his friendly and for the most part optimistic poetry contrasts with the cold and aloof demeanor he presented to his friends. The most important positive aspect of the magic gesture in the poetry is to be seen in the poet's attitude toward nature. It seems plain from an examination of the imagery of the poems that nature is for Wordsworth one aspect of his unconscious mother image. The magic gesture which he is never tired of dramatizing toward this mother image produces the emotions of joy and reverence which he feels in the presence of nature. The magic gesture is thus another way of saying: "It is impossible that I should be at enmity with mother when I am so obviously in harmony with her." But although this is the primary motivation for much of Wordsworth's finest poetry, it does not tell the whole story. The poet's introspective honesty in expressing his emotions brought him to reveal the negative aspect of the magic gesture too. This negative aspect appears obscurely in the earlier poems but becomes more evident in the later ones. It is this progress which it will be of interest to observe.

As an example of an early poem which is predominantly an expression of the positive magic gesture we may look first at *Lines Composed a Few Miles Above Tintern Abbey*. The poem opens with a description which includes several of the symbols which Wordsworth habitually uses to suggest his attachment to the unconscious pregenital mother image. There is first of all the river Wye itself which compares in importance with the river Duddon in the passage in the *Prelude* where Wordsworth is describing his infancy at Cockermouth—the very names have an oral significance! Then there are the springs and mountains from which the river flows. All three allude, unconsciously, to the breast as the dispenser of liquid nourishment. The scene is secluded and thus suggests the intimacy between mother and child, just as the landscape of mother earth is closely related to the quiet sky of Zeus-Ouranos. There are also some touches to suggest the awe which is due the mother as a superior power in the steepness of the cliffs and the wildness of the scene. Finally there may be a hint of the masochistic attachment to the mother in the mention of the "vagrant dwellers in the houseless the hedgegrows run wild, symbolize the infant abandoned by the mother; or the child whose aggression against the mother, in revenge for its abandonment, is turned against itself. But these latter hints of a rift between mother nature and her child are canceled out by Wordsworth's saying that:

> *these beauteous forms*
> *Through long absence, have not been to me*
> *As is a landscape to a blind man's eye.*

He is saying not only that he has not forgotten in times of loneliness the things which he once saw, but also that his eye is receptive to the sights which mother nature gives, just as the infant's mouth is receptive of nourishment. Hence the slightly out-of-the-ordinary reference to the blind man. The force of these unconscious memories of passive obedience to his mother give him tranquil restoration. They also have the effect of making him imitate the goodness of the mother in his own acts of kindness and love. Finally they produce in him:

> *that blessed mood,*
> *In which the burthen of the mystery,*
> *In which the heavy and the weary weight*
> *Of all this unintelligible world,*
> *Is lightened:*

By implication, then, there are times when mother nature is not by to prevent this weary weight from depressing us. Nevertheless, when her presence is felt, the weight is not only lightened (*n.b.* the play on the double sense of "lifted" and "made light" so that the eye can be fed), but we even show our gratitude by not needing to draw breath-nourishment from her profferred breast!

But though Wordsworth now speaks of an eye-mouth made quiet by the power of harmony, there is still the suggestion that all this may be but a vain belief. Furthermore the Wye, which is now first addressed by name, is termed a wanderer through the woods and this in turn suggests the elusive character of the stream which flows from mother's breast. There may also be an unconscious allusion to one of Wordsworth's earlier poems, *Margaret*, later known as *The Wanderer*. (It is the story of a bad mother who neglects her children and wanders about the countryside disconsolately searching for the husband who has abandoned her.) And as Wordsworth tries to recollect his first experience of the Wye valley he finds that he must do so

> *With gleams of half-extinguished thought*
> *With many recognitions dim and faint*
> *And something of a sad perplexity.*

Surely these are strange difficulties for one so close to mother nature. He
now alludes to the coarser pleasures of his boyish days which the *Prelude*
tells us included snaring woodcocks and robbing bird's nests, typical boyish
forms of aggression against the breast as symbolized in the bird. It appears
that this earlier experience with nature in this spot were not so tranquilly
passive as now, even though the memories which come now will be food for
future thought. For then he

> bounded o'er the mountains, by the sides
> Of deep rivers, and the lonely streams,
> Wherever nature led: more like a man
> Flying from something that he dreads, than one
> Who sought the thing he loved.

One is reminded by this of the passage in the *Prelude* where the young
Wordsworth rows across the lake in the moonlight and is frightened by the
uncanny appearance of a mountain peak—an unconscious reminiscence of
the breast. Then, he continues, the cataract haunted him and the mountain
and gloomy wood were an appetite to him—food for the eye alone. It is true
that these aching joys and dizzy raptures are thought of as a loss which the
poet does not mourn for since nature now gives other goods, but he cannot
forget them.

Among the new gifts which nature now gives him is the famous "still,
sad music of humanity." Nature, it seems, can also inflict suffering, for man
is not clearly distinguished from her other creations in this respect. And because of this fundamental unity among all creatures, even suffering is "music." Wordsworth may have arrived at this way of expressing his sanction
of masochistic suffering through the unconscious association of sounds-milk,
for we note a still further paradox in the fact that the music is "still," that
is, silent, and hence the absence of sounds-milk. From the difficult problem
of pain Wordsworth turns again to one of nature's more reassuring gifts:
the mystic sense of her very presence. Even this has a masochistic tinge for
it "disturbs" us, albeit with joy. It is to be found in the light of setting suns,
mother as earth or sea; the round ocean, mother's breast; the living air,
oral connotations of breathing; the blue sky, Zeus and Ouranos as partners
of earth; and finally it *rolls* through all things. The verb suggests that the
presence is really best symbolized by the motion of the river and the sea.
This is an important identification of the oral mother symbols of sea and
river with mother nature. For Wordsworth is again asserting the magic gesture positively. In spite of the remoteness and the pain which she gives, he
is *still* her lover and is well pleased to look upon her as his nurse, guide and

guardian. Nevertheless the landscape is not the only source of mother symbols on which he may rely. There is his sister Dorothy, who since she cannot be thought of as wife, is conveniently taken as mother. She is immediately associated with the river as symbol of the giving breast. Her wild eyes suggest his earlier, slightly more aggressive attitude toward mother nature, and he prays:

> *Oh! yet a little while*
> *May I behold in thee what I once was*
> *My dear, dear sister!*

The prayer may gain added significance if we remember that only a few years previous to this time Wordsworth narrowly escaped marriage with Annette Vallon, and only a few years were to elapse before he was to take Mary Hutchinson as his wife. Now it is his sister Dorothy who can afford the best object for his attachment to and identification with the pregenital mother image.

Thus in the concluding lines of the poem Wordsworth continues to strengthen the identification between nature and his sister and both are referred back to the pregenital mother image he is attempting to placate by means of the positive magic gesture. Thus nature leads him on from joy to joy, feeds his mind with lofty thoughts, and fortifies him against the wiles of the world. Since this is the case, therefore, he says, let the moon-mother shine on his sister and let the mountain-breast winds blow against her. Thus she too will realize that nature is beneficent, and more important still she will be a witness to the fact that he, Wordsworth, was unwearied in nature's service, had a warmer and holier love and deeper zeal for her than at first, and that she was more dear, both for her own sake and for his sister's sake. No disclaimer of hostility or demonstration of affection could be more emphatic. Surely the unconscious mother image must accept this evidence of good faith—and the implied reproach!

But the misgivings of which there is some evidence in *Tintern Abbey* were not to be downed. Two years later when Wordsworth wrote *Michael* they seem to have been expressed in a much stronger form. For the tragedy of this poem hinges in large part on the breakdown of the positive magic gesture and the consequent sense that man is betrayed by mother nature. As the poem opens we again have Wordsworth stressing the usual breast symbols: the brook and the mountain. But the tumult of the former and the steepness and rockiness of the latter together with the kite, a bird of prey, suggest that the mother image is less gracious than we found it in the

Wye valley. The utter solitude of the place where Michael lives seems to indicate that mother nature has become more remote from man here. Yet Wordsworth tells us that he is not interested in the shepherds, the characters of the story, for their own sake, but because of their relation to the fields and hills where they live, that is, their relation to mother nature. He also tells us that the passions he is about to describe are not his own, which suggests that the motivations of this story stem more directly from the unconscious than the magic gesture will ordinarily permit.

Michael, we are told, is a shepherd more than capable in his calling. He has phenomenal strength and this reminds us that he is named for the strongest of God's archangels. He has a peculiar knowledge of the winds foreboding storms and this enables him to tell when he must get to the mountains to take care of his sheep. But most important of all is the fact that Michael has an affection for his native fields, streams and rocks which amounts to a "pleasurable feeling of blind love." We are next told that he has a wife twenty years his junior and a son born in his old age—he is eighty-four when his son is eighteen. The family is an industrious one for the housewife spins late at night while husband and son help her to card the wool. This fact, to which Wordsworth devotes considerable attention, may be another hint that the mother symbol is hostile to the men. For the thread which she spins will be made into cloth which will in turn be used to deny the infant those voyeuristic sights which it so much desires, just as it desires milk for its mouth. The housewife is also said to place a lantern in the chimney piece to give light for the work and hence the cottage has gained the name of the "Evening Star." The evening star is the goddess Venus whose associations with love and war, in the *Aeneid*, for example, traditionally center around the breast symbol. It thus seems likely that Michael looks upon his wife more as the bad mother of the pregenital level of infantile experience than as a wife in the genital sense. Certainly Wordsworth tells us that the couple was neither gay nor cheerful and that Michael though he "must needs" love his wife really found his son more dear—not from instinctive tenderness but because a son gives the old man hope and certain "stirrings of inquietude."

So much affection is Michael said to have for his son that as an infant he often did him female service. The suggestion that Michael is unconsciously the boy's mother is further borne out by the relation of how the boy is reproved by the father when he disturbs the sheep who are being sheared under the clipping tree. The castration threat is unmistakable but the total context of the story suggests that it is on the oral rather than the oedipal level. It is bad mother who withdraws the breast from the infant's mouth rather than the jealous father who is at fault. The bad mother-father is responsible for putting the boy to work prematurely by making him an unmanageable staff for helping with the shepherding. Here, too, the boy does not always receive his hire of praise. But as he grows older the father's affection grows too and there seem to emanate from the boy feelings which give light to the sun and music to the wind. There may, indeed, be some homosexual overtones to the attachment between father and son which serve as a defense against the masochistic attachment to the bad-mother image, represented in the story by the austerity of nature as well as by Michael and the housewife. We remember that Milton's archangel Michael is hermaphrodite. But if so, Wordsworth does not objectify these hints in anything like the way Coleridge does in *The Ancient Mariner.*

An unexpected chance now intervenes. Michael is called upon to stand good for the debts of his brother's son which in terms of the symbolism of the story may mean that he is called upon to assume the role of the giving mother as opposed to the denying mother which he has been playing toward his own son. His first thought is to sell his patrimonial fields. But to do this would be tantamount to a rejection of mother nature, a voluntary rejection of the breast symbolized by his native hills. Such a rejection is prevented by the positive magic gesture which Michael and Wordsworth both make toward mother nature. Unconsciously the masochistic attachment is too strong and so it is determined to send the boy Luke away in order that he may earn the money in the city. Here again we have Michael playing the role of the denying mother toward his son, rejecting him in order that he may keep up his own façade of being on good terms with mother nature. The wife significantly is silent, i.e., she also plays the denying mother, at Michael's proposal though she treats herself to a fantastic daydream about the boy's possible success in trade. It is true that she later forbids the boy to go but she soon recovers heart and makes the necessary preparations. Michael himself, though ill at ease, seems positively eager that he shall go as soon as possible.

Before they part Michael takes Luke to Greenhead Ghyll and sitting down beside the tumultuous brook begins to recount fond memories of Luke's infancy. He tells how passively obedient he was at his mother's breast and how close he was to his father later. At this Luke bursts into tears. Michael goes on to relate how his fields were first encumbered with debt but how he succeeded in freeing them—again the positive magic gesture. Finally he tells him that he intends to build a sheepfold here and that he wishes Luke to lay the first stone. This symbolic act will help him to face the temptations of evil men when he gets out in the world. The fact that it does not do this shows us that here is Michael's second tragic error. For the building of the sheepfold in itself is an aggressive affront to mother nature. When the sheep wandered freely over the mountains they were like the milk that flows freely from the mother's breast. The move to pen them up suggests that mother is no longer to be trusted. No wonder Michael bursts into tears as Luke lays the first stone. The magic gesture has proved inadequate; mother is far more unrelenting than Michael supposed. For Luke goes wrong and flees beyond the seas, and Michael, though he still tries to build the sheepfold in defiance of the mother, often goes to the place and merely sits there with his dog—perhaps an allusion to the Dog Star in the constellation of Orion who was killed by the bad mother Hecate-Artemis—without lifting a stone. All of his efforts come to naught. After his death his land is sold for ploughland, a hint at its reversion to the normal level of heterosexual experience, and only the remnants of the unfinished sheepfold remain beside the brook.

In *Michael,* then, Wordsworth dramatizes the breakdown of the positive magic gesture toward mother nature. The action of the narrative, however, is not so tightly knit as it might be and Wordsworth's genius seems to have fitted him for a more meditative kind of poetry. When we turn to *Ode: Intimations of Immortality from Recollections of Early Childhood,* we see him in further difficulties in his attempt to assert the magic gesture. The epigraph for the *Ode* is from an earlier short poem of Wordsworth's of which he quotes only the last three lines:

> *The child is father of the man;*
> *And I could wish my days to be*
> *Bound each to each by natural piety.*

But the preceding lines are important, for they express Wordsworth's joy at seeing the rainbow; and the rainbow, according to Biblical tradition, is a promise that mother nature will not give too much liquid so as to drown her unsuspecting infants. She will, indeed, give just the right amount. This beneficent attitude of nature to man which is the aggressive giving of light-liquid as positive magic gesture and which the poet once felt so deeply, he now tells us he has lost. This sense of loss has even penetrated into the memories of the time when the oral breast-mother symbols—meadow, grove, stream, earth—for which he longs were wholly accessible. For these are said to be appareled in celestial light and the suggestion of clothing is already a hindrance to the voyeuristic eagerness with which the child longs for the breast. This same unconscious ambivalence creeps into the second stanza too. The promise of the rainbow comes, but then it also goes. The rose is lovely, but then it is also proud as Wordsworth tells in his poems *To the Small Celandine* and *To the Daisy*. The moon looks about her with delight, but only when the heavens are bare of her children the stars. Waters on a starry night, it is true, is just right; but the glorious birth of the sun carries more connotations of the aggressive Apollo-infant than is proper in a harmonious relation between mother and child.[2]

But though at the end of the second stanza Wordsworth says that a glory, i.e., the aggressive infant as the glorious sun, has passed from the earth, at the beginning of the third he reasserts his confidence in mother nature. The birds-breast sing, the lambs-milk bound, even the poet's thought of grief has been expelled by a "timely utterance"—presumably his poem *Resolution and Independence*. (In this poem the poet was cured of a fit of despondency—unconscious feeling of being abandoned by the mother image—by hearing an old leech-gatherer, whose wife and ten children are dead, say that he still perseveres in his trade even though the leeches are hard to find in the ponds. The leeches here symbolize the child clinging to the breast.) The poet accordingly hears the cataracts and the echoes in the mountains and feels the winds and the gaiety of earth. In the fourth stanza he continues his exuberance, but again the thought of his sullenness intrudes. It is strengthened by the mention of the children culling flowers, an image which suggests the genital more than the pregenital level of experience. There is further strengthening of the rift between the poet and nature in the association of the sun and its warm, aggressive rays with the babe leaping in its mother's arms; but the final disillusioning stroke comes at the sight of a tree—again an oral symbol—and a field-mother earth. The visionary gleam which delighted the eye, as milk from the breast delighted the lips, is gone.[3]

Some new attempt to establish the harmony between child and mother image is needed. Perhaps it can be done by the Platonic doctrine of pre-existence which asserts the immortality and divinity of the soul. This will have the advantage of exonerating the child from the guilt which attaches to its aggression against the mother image, for the soul comes from its divine state in a spotless condition. Accordingly the fifth stanza begins with various images minimizing the pain of separation. Our birth is a sleep, at which time the infant is not conscious of the mother's presence. Our life's star rises at the birth and thus departs from the horizon of the mother, but it has had its setting—approach to mother earth—elsewhere. Here the magic gesture again begins to break down for in the image that we come trailing clouds of glory some of the aggressiveness of the glorious sun begins to force itself upon us.

> *Heaven lies about us in our infancy!*
> *Shades of the prison house begin to close*
> *Upon the growing boy,*
> *But he beholds the light, and whence it flows,*
> *He sees it in his joy;*

It is as punishment for the guilt of this aggression that we are condemned to the prison house. One sees how far the poet has come from the time when he wrote *Tintern Abbey*. Then the world of mother nature was rapturously beautiful, not only to the child but to the grown man too. That the shift from the good-mother image to the bad should mean a shift from heavenly home (womb) to prison house (masochistic self-torture) is a tragic comment on human life. The rest of the stanza is dominated by this sense of the futility of escaping from the guilt which attaches to aggression against the mother image.

But the last line of the stanza tells us that the light-milk which radiates from mother is not wholly gone. What remains is the light of common day and this suggests the genital, as opposed to the pregenital level of experience —there are pejorative associations with-common woman, harlot, and heterosexual intercourse. We have already had a hint that this was to be one of the objections against adult life in the reference to the children culling flowers. Accordingly in stanza six we learn that earth (now the image of mother on the genital level) has pleasures of her own which seemingly cannot be shared by the infant on the pregenital level. They are yearnings in her own natural kind, that is, toward reproduction of the species. To attain this end, the mother must do all she can to make her "inmate" man forget the guilt of his aggression, i.e., his glories, against the pregenital mother image: the imperial palace where the little megalomaniac reigned supreme. The attainment of the genital level by the six-years' darling, approximately the age of the oedipal relationship, is now to be described in the seventh stanza. So the curious allusion to the child's pigmy size may be an inverted phallic suggestion. His mother's kisses now have a heterosexual meaning and the light upon him from his father's eyes carries with it the threat of oedipal aggression of father against son. The child begins to take cognizance of an

objective world of which he knew nothing on the pregenital level. He cele-
brates his wedding and realizes the meaning of death. Wordsworth rightly
sees that all these higher levels of experience depend on imitation, an imitation which is impossible so long as the child remains masochistically attached to the pregenital mother image.

After this description of the child's attainment of maturity the poet
begins the eighth stanza in a spirit of confidence. He speaks of the soul's immensity and terms the child a mighty prophet and blessed seer. But all is
not well yet.

> *Thou best philosopher, who yet dost keep*
> *Thy heritage, thou eye among the blind,*
> *That, deaf and silent, read'st the eternal deep,*
> *Haunted forever by the eternal mind,—*

Perhaps the child is a philosopher in the sense that he is a Stoic born to
pain—as Dr. Johnson said that he tried hard to be a philosopher, but cheer-
fulness always kept breaking in! Moreover the child is an eye-mouth that
reads the eternal deep, the ocean of the pregenital mother. There are dis-
turbing overtones in the fact that he is *haunted* by the eternal mind and
that as adults we are lost in the darkness of the grave, hardly an optimistic
way of describing normal heterosexual development since the grave is probably a pejorative reference to the feminine genitals. There are still more
ominous connotations in the statement that our immortality—attachment
to the pregenital mother—broods over us like master over slave. The aggression against the mother image is now stated by saying that the child is glorious in his might and the masochistic form of this aggression when it is
turned against the self appears in the question:

> *Why with such earnestness dost thou provoke*
> *The years to bring the inevitable yoke,*
> *Thus blindly with thy blessedness at strife?*

In such masochistic conflict the mother is cold and the child adopts the attitude of an other-worldly ascetic. All this fits in neatly with the other-
worldly aspects of Platonism.

But at the beginning of stanza nine the poet once more tries to establish the original magic gesture. In words that remind us of *Tintern Abbey*
he tells us that "the thought of our past years in me doth breed perpetual
benediction." But it is not the simple creed of childhood, that is, not for the
positive magic gesture toward the pregenital mother image that he rejoices.
Rather it is:

> *those obstinate questionings*
> *Of sense and outward things,*
> *Fallings from us, vanishings;*
> *Blank misgivings of a creature*
> *Moving about in worlds not realised,*

These feelings, which describe the child's reaction to the denying-mother image and hence form the basis of the negative magic gesture, are now termed the child's first affections and the fountain light of all our day. They are something quite different from the joyful emotions which formed the basis of the positive magic gesture and which were celebrated in *Tintern Abbey*. They are the feelings which made Michael create his own tragedy and which made Wordsworth celebrate Duty as the "stern daughter of the voice of God." They can make our noisy years seem moments in the eternal silence of the denying mother and can recall to us the immortal sea whose mighty waters have the power to inspire dread, though as children we may not realize how mighty the mother image really is.

And yet once more in stanza ten the poet expresses the positive magic gesture and is with the lambs and birds in thought at least, though again he soon admits that the radiance of the mother image is forever taken from his sight. Now he speaks wistfully of finding strength in primal sympathy, though he cannot quite believe it. Strength now comes from the aggressive relation which, when turned against the self, brings those strangely soothing thoughts that spring out of human suffering! The years now bring the philosophic mind which is plainly that of a Stoic. Well may the poet, in the concluding stanza, plead that there may be no severing of his love and the fountains and the hills. He says that he has relinquished only one delight, that is, the positive magic gesture. He says he loves the brooks even more than when he tripped as lightly as they—and thus betrays that he loves them in a very different fashion now. The clouds that gather now around the setting sun, symbol of the reconciliation of infantile aggression with the mother image, take a sober coloring from an eye that hath kept watch over man's mortality—that is, even here there is no reconciliation. Now the meanest flower, with all its connotations of the heterosexual level of experience which is denied to the individual attached to the pregenital mother image, can give thoughts that do often lie too deep for tears. Thus the ode unconsciously ends on a note of the deepest tragedy. It is a grief deeper than tears can express which the poet feels as a result of his estrangement from his infantile recollections of immortality. This is the child inconsolable for the loss of its mother.

In the three poems which have been discussed so far we have seen several important changes in Wordsworth's use of the magic gesture. In *Tintern Abbey* it is vigorously asserted in its most positive form though not without some misgivings. In *Michael* it already begins to show itself in its negative form although the positive form is still strong enough to determine the course of the plot and the tragic outcome of the story. In *Ode: Intimations of Immortality* the positive magic gesture seems to be wholly abandoned though recollections of it remain in the poet's mind and make his acceptance of the negative gesture more poignantly painful. When we turn to *Laodamia*, written some ten years more or less after the *Ode*, we find Wordsworth's acceptance of the negative magic gesture complete with little or no trace of the positive form remaining. Needless to say this indication of the direction of change from positive to negative magic gesture does not mean that Wordsworth did not write poems late in life which express the positive magic gesture. What is indicated is a general trend in Wordsworth's attitude toward nature, a trend which has long been known and studied from other points of view.

It is perhaps significant that in dramatizing the negative magic gesture Wordsworth should turn to a story which has as its background the *Iliad*. For the *Iliad* is the tragedy of Achilles whose homosexual love for Patroclus is a part of the pregenital masochistic aggression against the mother image. The *Iliad* may thus be looked upon as a poem which gives the appropriate background to the negative magic gesture. Its pessimism is farthest removed from the optimism of *Tintern Abbey,* and this is also the case with *Laodamia.* Wordsworth's poem opens with Laodamia speaking—she is the image of the giving mother, not only on the pregenital but also on the genital level—and telling us that she has made a plea to Jove, the classical father principle and representative of the oedipus complex on the genital level, to return her dead husband Protesilaus. But the mention of the fact that she has made a sacrifice and that her husband was slaughtered in battle also hints at the strong masochistic elements which attach to the pregenital level of experience. That Laodamia is the image of the giving mother is suggested by the second stanza where she is compared to the sun emerging from a cloud—infantile aggression projected onto the image of the denying mother-cloud. Her eye and bosom, mouth-breast, are said to expand and heave, and there may even be a hint of phallic symbolism on the genital level in the words:

> her stature grows;
> And she expects the issue in repose.

But when Protesilaus appears, Laodamia's emotions are highly ambivalent. She *perceives* him (passive relation of wife to husband) with terror, but *looks* upon him (active relation of mother to son) with joy and thus already forebodes the fact that Protesilaus is capable only on the pregenital level of experience. This is borne out by his being led by Hermes, the winged god who with Aphrodite is the father of the original hermaphrodite. Hermes now touches her with his wand, perhaps in order to calm her fear of her husband's homosexual propensities, for these will soon be apparent, and tells her that Jove has granted her wish for the short space of three hours. At this Laodamia springs forward in order to clasp her waiting spouse but succeeds only in tearing him into pieces which reunite as she withdraws. Thus she symbolizes the pregenital fantasy of the devouring mother! She says that now since Hermes is gone—vainly thinking perhaps that he alone exercises the homosexual influence—Protesilaus must confirm the vision with his voice, that is, he must identify with the giving mother on the genital level. For then, she adds, the floor (perhaps a pejorative allusion to the lowness of heterosexual relations) will rejoice.

But Protesilaus coldly repulses her, thus identifying with the denying mother, by saying that Jove has not left his gifts imperfect. This may mean that he does not need to complete himself in the opposite sex, and he adds that he has been sent as a reward for his fearless virtue, perhaps a hint at the aggressive basis of the homosexual rejection of the mother image. He says that the Delphic oracle—again Apollo, the archer god of pregenital aggression—foretold that the first Greek to land at Troy must die. Protesilaus was the first, voluntarily leaping from his ship (ocean as giving mother) onto the sandy (dry, denying mother) beach to be killed by Hector who also kills Achilles' homosexual friend Patroclus. He terms the Trojan war a generous cause and says that he was self-devoted to it—an attitude which contrasts sharply with Wordsworth's youthful pacifism.

Laodamia's reply shows that she is already beginning to weaken in her heterosexual demands. She says brokenly that during the war he found a nobler counselor than her heart. Nevertheless she adds that now Jove, who brings him back to her has decreed that he shall elude the malice of the grave—and perhaps here she refers not to the grave's body-destroying power but rather the fear of the feminine genitals which it symbolizes. She speaks of his redundant locks which are not only luxurious but also superflous, thus suggesting castration, and remarks on the rosy color of his lips. The mention of the Thessalian air recalls the witches for which that region was famous and suggests in turn the bad-mother image. Finally she proposes that he join her upon the nuptial couch, that is, that he identify with the giving mother instead of the denying image. At this

> *Jove frowned in heaven: the conscious Parcae threw*
> *Upon the roseate lips a Stygian hue.*

But it is not clear whether Jove frowns at the forwardness of Laodamia or at the refusal of Protesilaus. The Parcae, also images of the denying mother as spinner and shearer, by making pale the hero's lips, forbid the heterosexual union, and it is to be noted that the change is wrought in the man and not in the woman—a fact which suggests that the guilt lies with him.

Protesilaus now tells Laodamia that his doom is past and hence he is not capable of heterosexual love. Earth-mother, he says, destroys those raptures, while in Erebus only calm pleasures and majestic pains are to be found—a conception of the other world quite different from that of Homer, Vergil, Dante, or Milton. With Victorian stuffiness he adds that the gods approve the depth and not the tumult of the soul and we remember that *Tintern Abbey* approved both the depth and tumult. Moreover, he says that Laodamia must bear his parting meekly—advice which reminds us of Ruskin's treatment of Effie Gray. But Laodamia is not so easily put off. She reminds him of that great oedipal hero Hercules rescuing Alcestis from a monster-father. Her second example is less fortunately chosen and shows that she is weakening again. It is Medea, the murderess of her children, though Laodamia cites Ovid's version of the renewal of Aeson rather than the version in which he is killed by her. She reminds him that

> *mightier far*
> *Than strength of nerve and sinew, or the sway*
> *Of magic potent over sun and star,*
> *Is love, though oft to agony distrest,*
> *And though his favorite seat be feeble woman's breast.*

She thus stresses the giving mother's breast and its power over the aggressive pregenital symbols of sun and star.

But at this point Protesilaus commands silence and Laodamia fatally acquiesces, though seemingly calmed and cheered. Yet her action means that she abandons her role as giving mother. Wordsworth continues to tell us at second hand that Protesilaus lectures Laodamia on the almost insufferable purity of the other world. He speaks of the love which only spirits feel and here the allusion to Milton's hermaphroditic angels is unmistakable. He says the streams, air, and light—all symbols of nourishment from the breast—are there more pure than on earth. The sun is, indeed, unworthy to shine there. And now Protesilaus begins to speak again and stresses the nobility of his self-sacrificing action in being killed first at Troy. He tells of the fleet's being detained at Aulis by Diana, bad mother who demands the sacrifice of Iphigenia; and how he meditates on the oracle while on the silent sea. He thinks of the joys he has shared with his wife: fountains, flowers, new-planned cities, unfinished towers, all symbols (with the exception of the flowers) of unattained genital maturity. He thinks of the indignity of being accused by the foe of cowardice. And thus thinking he has justified himself he turns to attack Laodamia for her "irrational" passion. He says that Laodamia should

> Learn, by a mortal yearning, to ascend—
> Seeking a higher object. Love was given,
> Encouraged, sanctioned, chiefly for that end;
> For this the passion to excess was driven—
> That self might be annulled: her bondage prove
> The fetters of a dream, opposed to love.—

It is thus the Platonic and ascetic (homosexual and masochistic) ideal of love which he recommends. Heterosexual love, which is the basis of the preservation of the species, is called a bondage, fetters of a dream which dissipates.

Well may Laodamia shriek at the appearance of Hermes now. But Protesilaus departs silently for his unearthly home, leaving Laodamia lifeless upon the floor. Wordsworth tells us that the hero's mission, which was presumably to convert Laodamia from coarse heterosexual love to the more refined homosexual type, has been in vain. But there is a sense in which this supposed mission of Protesilaus is a hoax. After all he was not sent but summoned by Jove and Laodamia. Furthermore it is not he who has failed to convince his wife, but she who has failed to win him. The justice of the gods, therefore, which decrees that she shall not gather flowers among the dead, that is, engage in heterosexual union with her spouse, is meted out because she has abandoned heterosexuality and acquiesced in the lofty sterile homosexuality of Protesilaus. Perhaps it is for this reason that Wordsworth added the last stanza in which Protesilaus, in spite of all his noble purity, also receives a symbolic punishment quite as typical of his crime as that of Laodamia. The spiry trees, phallic symbols, which grow from his tomb wither every time their tops are high enough to see the walls of Troy which is perhaps a symbol of the productive life of the family on the genital level—Priam and his fifty sons and fifty daughters. It is this detail which Wordsworth said in a note first gave him the idea for the poem and thus indicated, perhaps, his fundamental honesty in realizing that Protesilaus is the real culprit. In any case, the negative magic gesture which completely rejects the bad-mother image without accepting any good from her is now fully expressed.

Biographical facts concerning Wordsworth's youth are scanty, but there is some evidence that he may have been suffering from an unconscious conflict with his mother. He was born in 1770, his brother Richard having been born in 1768. His sister Dorothy was born in 1771, John in 1772, and Christopher in 1774. In his *Autobiographical Memoranda* he says that an intimate friend of his mother once told him that he was the only one of five children about whose future life she was anxious.

The cause of this was that I was of a stiff, moody, and violent temper; so much so that I remember once going into the attic of my grandfather's house at Penrith, upon some indignity having been put upon me, with an intention of destroying myself with one of the foils which I knew was kept there. I took the foil in my hand, but my heart failed.

This anecdote gains added meaning if we remember that psychoanalysis has shown that suicide is unconsciously an attempt to attack some hated psychic object which the individual does not dare attack in reality. In Wordsworth's case the aggression seems to be directed against the mother —probably as a defense against a masochistic tendency which is evident in the "indignity" mentioned. Another anecdote related by Wordsworth in this same paper seems to confirm this supposition.

While I was at my grandfather's house at Penrith, along with my eldest brother, Richard, we were whipping tops together in the large drawing room, on which the carpet was only laid down upon particular occasions. The walls were hung round with family pictures, and I said to my brother, "Dare you strike your whip through that old lady's petticoat?" He replied, "No, I won't." "Then," I said, "here goes!" and I struck my lash through her hooped petticoat; for which, no doubt, though I have forgotten it, I was properly punished. . . . But possibly from some want of judgment in punishments inflicted, I had become perverse and obstinate in defying chastisement, and rather proud of it than otherwise.

His mother died when he was eight years old, as Wordsworth almost facetiously says "of a decline, brought on by a cold, in consequence of being put, at a friend's house in London, in what used to be called 'a best bedroom.' " At this time the family was dispersed and William was sent to

Hawkshead grammar school. Contrary to expectation we learn from the *Autobiographical Memoranda* that these earliest days at school "were happy ones, chiefly because I was left at liberty."

The most interesting and the most mysterious episode in Wordsworth's biography is his affair with Annete Vallon. Prior to this time he seems to have had no serious attachments to women. He had several close male friends, though even these relationships were not very passionate. There are, however, various indications that his masochistic tendencies were still in evidence. Among these we may note his plagiarism of certain passages describing his travels through the Alps from a book by Ramond de Carbonierres. It was in 1792 that he met and wooed Annette Vallon. But before she had given birth to his daughter, Wordsworth was in Paris and from thence he went to England. Nine years were to pass before he was to see her again, and then it would be on the eve of his marriage to another woman. Mr. Herbert Read and others have tried to find the reason for this strange desertion of the woman who should have been his wife in the political views which Wordsworth held at this time and which made it impossible for him to remain in France or to return there until it was too late to patch up his waning love for Annette. However valid these speculations may be, I think there is room for a psychological interpretation of the event. If we may assume that Wordsworth had a strong unconscious masochistic attachment to the mother image, then the aggressive character of his abandonment of Annette becomes more understandable. It is a defensive denial of his passivity in relation to women, an attempt at brutality in order to prove that he does not want to be mistreated.

The plausibility of this interpretation is heightened by the fact, mentioned by Mr. Read, that Wordsworth himself says he had only a pseudo interest in politics when in France at this time. He was indeed more interested in a sentimental picture of the Virgin by Charles Le Brun of which he later wrote:

> *A beauty exquisitely wrought, with hair*
> *Dishevelled, gleaming eyes, and rueful cheek*
> *Pale and bedropped with overflowing tears.*

May not the interest in this picture indicate that Wordsworth was attempting to reverse the roles from cruel mother—persecuted son to persecuted mother—(the Virgin and Annette) cruel son? It is true that this reversal was only momentarily successful, for Wordsworth soon lost his sadistically tinged love for Annette and her war-torn country. In place of it he allowed himself to think of France as a monster of iniquity and as Mr. Read sug-

gests he may unconsciously have identified France (personified as the feminine goddess of Reason) with Annette. If so, we have another reason why
he could not, ten years later when he did meet her once more, find any love
in his heart for her. To do so would have been to face his masochistic attachment to her in its true proportions. His rejection of her was, then, a
pseudo-aggressive defense against his passivity. Indeed something of this
same pattern seems to have been repeated when, after marrying Mary
Hutchinson in 1802, he and his sister Dorothy and Coleridge departed for a
tour of the Highlands almost immediately after Mary had risen from the
childbed of their first child. Here again we see the need to flee and hence
reject the object of his affection, though now, of course, it appears in a
much less drastic form.

Mr. Read also points out that the period of Wordsworth's finest literary productivity coincides with the years which are limited by his affair
with Annette on the one hand and the first five years of his marriage on the
other. Now if we recall that writing may be considered as a pseudo-aggressive defense against the unconscious mother image we may see further significance in the fact that Wordsworth was most creative when he was trying
to maintain his pseudo-aggressive defense with respect to Annette Vallon.
The poetry of this period has a vitality which the later poetry lacks, partly
because in it he could act out the positive side of his magic gesture—"This
is how mother should have treated me"—while he was acting the negative
side in real life. In later life Wordsworth seems to have thoroughly repressed his conscious knowledge of his affair with Annette. (Ellis Yarnall
while interviewing Wordsworth in 1847 said: "Addressing Mrs. Wordsworth he said, 'I wonder how I came to stay there (i.e., at Orleans in September 1792) so long, and at a period so exciting.") And as the chances for
the negative magic gesture diminished in real life, so too the chances for the
positive magic gesture diminished in poetry. Mr. Read also points out that
Wordsworth after this single creative period began to suffer from the inhibiting effects of writer's block—again an indication that the pseudo-aggressive defense was being rejected more and more by the unconscious conscience.

IV

KEATS

The Eve of St. Agnes • *La Belle Dame Sans Merci* • *Lamia*

FROM the point of view of expressing unconscious conflicts, the second generation of Romantic poets—Keats, Byron, and Shelley—had a great advantage over the first. In Wordsworth and Coleridge they could find unconscious symbols and patterns expressed in language which was congenial to their mode of feeling. This may help to explain the more elaborate style and complication of action which one finds in the later poets. Perhaps, too, it may be more than a coincidence that the three later poets were all cut short in their careers by early death whereas Wordsworth and Coleridge survived them by many years. It is certainly true that while Byron, Keats, and Shelley learned a great deal from their predecessors, they could not accept the adjustments which they had made. Keats, for example, was early under the influence of Wordsworth and was temperamentally more akin to him than to Coleridge. His *Endymion*, however different its style may be from that of Wordsworth, is psychologically very close to Wordsworth's attempt to solve the unconscious conflict with the pregenital mother image by means of a magic gesture. The attitude of Endymion toward Cynthia, the moon goddess who represents the pregenital mother image, is typically that of Wordsworth toward nature. It is again a way of saying: "This is how I wanted to be worshiped and adored." But the extreme dejection of Endymion when the moon goddess leaves him suggests the unconscious ambivalence which underlies this attitude of adoration. The strange inability of Endymion to adjust himself to an earthly mistress, Phoebe, who is obviously the mother image on the genital level, also hints at the unconscious ambivalence toward the pregenital mother. Keats ends the story by having

Cynthia and Phoebe turn out to be the same person and while this suggests the point that they are both mother images on different levels, it does not carry the psychological conviction which it should. It is, however, forced on Keats by the attitude of the positive magic gesture which he has adopted.

It is significant, however, that Keats cannot rest content with this use of the magic gesture. In the following year he attempted to express a castration theme in *Isabella, or the Pot of Basil*. The two wicked brothers are perhaps attempts to dramatize an oedipal father figure, but it is important that the actual beheading of Lorenzo is accomplished by Isabella and not by the brothers. This may be an indication that the castration Keats is interested in is not on the oedipal but on the oral level. The confusion between oral and genital castration, neither of which is clearly conceived or worked out, may account for some of Keats' dissatisfaction with his version of the story. There is a further attempt to treat the oedipal theme in the two versions of *Hyperion*. It is significant that here too Keats centers his attention on the archer sun god who is a type of pre-oedipal aggression, and that he proposed to dramatize the change from mere blind aggression in Hyperion to intelligent, foresighted aggression in Apollo. The inability to accomplish this feat in reality, as well as the explicitly oedipal background in the revolt of Jupiter against his father Saturn, may have been one of the psychological motivations for the abandonment of the epic before much of it had been accomplished. But the important thing about both these poems is that they show that Keats is not content with a merely static magic gesture toward the mother image. He has now begun to dramatize his defense against the conflict in terms which imply more action than appeared in *Endymion*.

In *The Eve of St. Agnes* one sees one of these defensive dramatizations which succeeds better than any of the earlier attempts. In it Keats asserts the importance and primacy of the genital level of experience. But in order to achieve this assertion he has to minimize the dangers of the pregenital level to such an extent that an air of unreality is thrown over the action of the poem. Denying the existence of a conflict, though he does not wholly succeed in this even temporarily, is not the same as overcoming it. However, the fact that Keats has not forgotten the importance of the masochistic attachment to the mother image appears from the first four stanzas of the poem. Here we have the picture of the ascetic beadsman freezing in his devotions to the mother image of the Virgin. For the beadsman is not merely "atmosphere." Without this preliminary declaration that the mother not only denies all pleasure but even the warmth which would signify some last flames of the long-forbidden love, Keats would not be able to dramatize Porphyro's winning of Madeline on the genital level of experience. Since the beadsman represents extreme aggression turned against the self as a defense, the extremity of passive submission to the mother image, Keats can mobilize a further defense against the already defensive beadsman in the figure of Porphyro, whose more normal relation to the mother image will tend to nullify the admission of guilt in the beadsman. The identification of the beadsman with the pregenital denying mother is suggested by such details as the silence of the flock in wooly fold, the knights and ladies praying in dumb oratories, and particularly in the fact that Keats forbids him to weep:

> *. . . scarce three steps, ere Music's golden tongue*
> *Flattered to tears this aged man and poor;*
> *But no—already had his death bell rung;*
> *The joys of all his life were said and sung:*
> *His was harsh penance on St. Agnes' Eve:*

There is, indeed, some evidence to suggest that the music and the festivities which are going on in the castle represent the oedipal level of experience.[1] The hostility of the father image is to be seen in the snarling of the trumpets, the comparison of the music to a god in pain and the mention of the fact that Madeline walks amid looks of defiance, hate and scorn. Furthermore, there seems to be a certain dwarfish Hildebrand and a Lord Maurice who are ringleaders in a blood feud against Porphyro's family. These hyena foemen are ready to draw their swords *(n.b.* the use of the oedipal weapon as opposed to the long distance pre-oedipal spears and bows) in the defense of the rights of the father against the interloping son. It is also true that Keats seems to conceive of the tradition of St. Agnes' Eve in terms of the overcoming of the denying mother image. There are concessions to her, such as going to bed supperless, but this is only so as to be fed later with a sight of the beloved. It is noted that it is part of the tradition that lambs are presented to the saint on this evening unshorn, and if we recollect that both castration (the shears) and denial of voyeuristic orality (weaving the shorn wool into cloth) are signs of the denying mother we can see how St. Agnes is being used as a defense against that denying mother. There is a similar hint in the curious phrase in which Keats says that the portal doors, an obvious feminine symbol, are buttressed from moonlight: that is, they are protected from the bad-mother symbol of the moon. The door symbols, indeed, seem to be quite specifically related to the genital level of experience, as when Porphyro's plume is so lofty that it brushes the cobwebs from the arch of the portal.

The description of old Angela, whose name and that of St. Agnes suggest each other, also implies that Keats is turning a denying-mother image into a giving-mother image who is to lend her gracious aid to Porphyro's project. We first see her shuffling along with an ivory-headed wand which reminds us of the great classical prototype of the phallic mother: Circe. It is she who turned Odysseus' men into pregenital suckling pigs without courage or strength. Angela, too, at first is only concerned to send Porphyro away as quickly as possible. Moreover, she takes him into a little moonlit room whose chill and silence again suggest the denying mother. Porphyro is not abashed, however, and even employs an oath—by St. Agnes' holy loom—which alludes to the denying mother. Angela in her turn alludes to the dangers of oedipal rivalry and says that he must be able to hold water in a witch's sieve: that is, play or know the trick of the denying mother, if he is to remain safe. But the ambivalent feelings with which Keats regards her are seen in her remark that Madeline is being deceived by good angels in hoping for a sight of her lover. This causes her to laugh feebly in the languid moon and thus suggest the waning influence of the bad mother. Yet this grimace makes Porphyro think of her as an aged crone keeping closed a book of riddles in the chimney nook—again the denying mother; and he knows how to counteract this denial first with tears, giving, on hearing of Madeline's vigil and then with the thought of his own appearance in her bedchamber, a thought which comes to him like a full-blown rose. This proposal, of course, strikes Angela as both cruel and impious—in spite of her willingness to help him. But Porphyro insists that if he looks with ruffian passion on her face he will arouse his foemen and beard them as if they were lions or wolves—again the oedipal motif. The mention of this sort of violence is sufficient to win over Angela, and Keats suggests at this point that there is some connection between this night and that on which Merlin paid his Demon all his monstrous debt: that is, to make the comparison explicit, Angela is an embodiment of the pregenital Super Ego which denies genital pleasure but which Porphyro has now temporarily succeeded in paying off.

Angela now hurries off to provide the delicacies which are to symbolize the consummation of the lovers' union. Madeline herself lights her way downstairs as if Keats wanted to show that she and Angela are to be identified in the change from pregenital to genital mother image. Thus when she approaches her chamber she is called a ring dove, that is, a breast symbol, but as she enters, the taper which she bears and which suggests Angela's ivory wand, goes out, its smoke dying in the pallid moonshine to show that the moon herself takes cognizance of the impending event. There is also an allusion to the death of a nightingale whose legendary prototype, Philomela, is again a symbol of the negative oedipal son in that she is attacked by the sadistic Tereus. The scene which follows where Madeline kneels before the stained-glass window is again symbolic of her entry into womanhood. The fruits, flowers, and the diamonded windowpanes are sanctioned by the scutcheon of her ancestors, parent images who were kings and queens. The rays of the wintry moon-mother when passed through this window are warmed and throw their light upon Madeline's breast which is now no longer an object of dread. Rose bloom falls on her hands, her silver cross is softened by amethyst. Her hair, a symbol of sexual potency, is like glory. She seems like an angel except that she has no wings, that is, she is not to be associated with those bird-breast hermaphrodite angels of Milton's *Paradise Lost*. As she moves to her bed she dare not look behind—as at pagan sacrifices placating Hecate—for fear of breaking the charm.

It is true that there are certain faint echoes of the pregenital past in this description. The colors in the window are compared to those in the tiger moth's wings and the mention of the tiger as devouring-mother symbol has an ominous sound. Then, too, Madeline disrobed among her gowns is compared to a mermaid in seaweed and this again suggests the pregenital level of experience. But these are only passing references and the sensuous description of Madeline's sleep with its poppied warmth, its praying paynims, and its image of the full-blown rose closing to a bud again all prelude the coming union of the lovers. As Porphyro steps from his hiding place the parent symbols are once more alluded to. But the moon is now more faded than before and the drum, clarion, and clarinet—all father symbols—are heard momentarily and then no more. He now sets out the table and

> *. . . from forth the closest brought a heap*
> *Of candied apple, quince, and plum, and gourd;*
> *With jellies soother than the creamy curd,*
> *And lucent syrops, tinct with cinnamon;*
> *Manna and dates, in argosy transferred*
> *From Fez; and spiced dainties, every one,*
> *From silken Samarcand to cedared Lebanon.*

Here again the ambiguity between genital and pregenital levels is apparent. Eating is, of course, a common dream symbol for sexual intercourse but it also carries with it connotations of the oral, pregenital level. But Keats makes his intention clear with his allusions to the freighted argosies-womb, and cedared Lebanon-phallus. So, too, the perfume of the food is said to warm the chilly room.

Still Porphyro himself has not conquered the bad pregenital mother image, as Madeline's vespers before the window have helped her to. When he speaks, he calls her a seraph, and says that he will be the hermit to her heaven, thus showing that he conceives of their relationship in terms of an ascetic, masochistic attachment. As he lays his unnerved arm on her pillow, he finds it as impossible to awaken her as to melt a frozen stream. The denying-mother image again comes to the fore as the moonlight gleams over the salvers and the fringe of the carpet. Porphyro's woofed fantasies suggest the symbol of the weaver who denies voyeuristic sights. In his extremity he takes up the lute and sings the ballad of *La Belle Dame Sans Merci*. Though Keats says it is a ballad long since mute, it is precisely by making Porphyro give utterance to this unique expression of the denying-mother image that he is capable of surmounting its inhibiting effect. It is possible that Keats' own poem of this title which he composed a few months later was already in his mind. It will therefore be worthwhile to review the contents of this poem for the light which it will shed on *St. Agnes.*

In this ballad the images which depict the denying mother are expressed in the clearest and most striking style. The sedge which has withered from the dried-up lake, the birds-breast which no longer give forth song, the squirrel which has taken all the nuts, a hint at castration, and the harvest which robs the earth of its fruitfulness, even the withering lily and the fading rose on the knight's face, suggest the dreadful, denying mother. La Belle Dame herself is a fairy creature whose long hair and light foot suggest the phallic mother, and whose singing is described as sweet moan. More important still is that she feeds the knight her sweet roots (breast) and her wild honey (milk) and in language strange says "I love thee true." But even here the defense is not lacking for the knight seemingly attempts to deny his passive role by saying that it is he who shuts her eyes and kisses her asleep and thus suggests that his love for her is on a genital level rather than the pregenital. But the cold hillside of the denying breast and the apparition of the starved victims of La Belle Dame shows plainly that the poem is an expression of the masochistic attachment to the denying-mother image in which the infant tries to put the blame on the mother for starving him.

> I saw pale kings, and princes too,
>   Pale warriors, death-pale were they all:
> Who cried—"La Belle Dame sans merci
>   Hath thee in thrall!"

I saw their starved lips in the gloom
With horrid warning gaped wide,
And I awoke, and found me here
On the cold hill side.

The relevance of this ballad to *St. Agnes* is clear when we see that Prophyro is to be identified with the knight and Madeline with La Belle Dame. For she, like La Belle Dame, makes soft moan upon hearing the ballad, and he, when she awakens, sinks on his knees, pale as sculptured stone and thus recalls the knight enthralled to La Belle Dame—or her more ancient prototype, the Medusa.

However, Madeline's first reaction upon awakening is to weep and moan forth witless words when she sees the discrepancy between the Porphyro of her dream and that which she sees kneeling beside her embodying the image of the denying mother. For Porphyro at first cannot move or speak, but Madeline's tears and words, together with the ballad which he has just sung, break the spell which the denying-mother image has over him. Now at last the union of the two lovers is possible and Keats tells us that

. . . he arose,
Ethereal, flushed, and like a throbbing star
Seen mid the sapphire heaven's deep repose;
Into her dream he melted, as the rose
Blendeth its odor with the violet—

So complete is their identification since Porphyro's name in Greek means purple. And yet even at this point the lovers are not permitted to forget the dangers from which they have presumably escaped. *St. Agnes'* moon has set and thus the image of the bad mother has vanished, but the winter sleet, love's alarum, continues to patter on the windowpane. It is significant that these icy gusts do not signify the oedipal dangers of the foemen to Porphyro, but rather the denying mother again. It is for this reason that Madeline still fears that she will be abandoned by Porphyro as a dove forlorn and lost. It is for this reason, too, that Porphyro says that he will be her vassal and no longer a famished pilgrim to her shrine nor, as before, a hermit to her heaven. Thus he rejects the ascetic, masochistic attachment for the familial, feudal principle. There is thus a progression from the homosexual to the heterosexual basis for love. And it is because of the progression that Porphyro can assure Madeline that the storm is only an elfin storm from fairyland.

The concluding stanzas of the poem are occupied with showing that the symbols of oral regression are completely overcome. The dragons of the phallic mother are all asleep, their spears—no longer oedipal swords—harmless as the hawk-breast which flutters as the arras is whipped by the wind of passion. The porter and the oedipal kinsmen have succumbed to the oral desire for drink and lie in a drunken stupor and the bloodhound which guards the gate lets the lovers pass without a difficulty. It is now the Baron as oedipal father figure who dreams of witches, demons, and coffin worms—all pre-oedipal mother figures. But though they threaten him they are harmless for the lovers, since the last lines of the poem tell us that Angela and the beadsman both die that very night. Yet one notices that the lovers themselves do not bring about the dissolution of these symbols of the denying mother and the unconscious masochistic attachment to her.[2] The poet is arranging things to suit their needs and this perhaps accounts to some extent for the air of unreality which pervades the poem. The pre-oedipal conflict has not been mastered. It has only been temporarily exorcised.

In *Lamia* Keats makes a bolder attempt to express the heart of the unconscious conflict with the pre-oedipal mother image. For Lamia, the serpent woman, plays the same role which Angela, the phallic-mother image, played in *St. Agnes*. Just as the successful elopement of Porphyro and Madeline might be considered as a defense against the conflict with the phallic mother, so the search of Hermes for the elusive nymph may be considered a defense against the now more prominently displayed conflict with the Lamia. Thus the effectiveness of the defense in *St. Agnes* turns upon the willingness of old Angela to be favorable to Porphyro's desires. Likewise the success of Hermes' search for his nymph is made dependent on the Lamia's revealing her to him. Keats has thus recognized that the image of the phallic mother needs more careful study than the treatment accorded her in the figure of Angela. In *Lamia*, consequently, most of the story is concerned with exploring this conflict directly, and the defense sketched in the Hermes episode is given only in order to ensure the proper perspective. Nevertheless Keats needs this defense, which incidentally is not part of the original story in Burton, in order to assert his allegiance to the primacy of genital over pregenital experience. He can explore the intricacies of the pregenital level only after he has paid his respects to the genital level.

There are several hints that Keats is attempting to distinguish between these two levels of experience in the first episode of the poem. He begins by calling to mind the difference between medieval and classical folk lore and his choice of faery brood to suggest the familial principle and faun and dryad to suggest the pre-oedipal level may thus be significant. The classical period, however, is not strictly equated with the pregenital level. Hermes, who as one of the few winged gods on Olympus carries with him associations of the breast complex, nevertheless steals away from the paternal eye of Jove bent on amorous theft, that is, an oedipal adventure. Thus in his search for the nymph he characteristically flies from vàle to vale, wood to wood, breathing upon the flowers his passion knew. But there are also pregenital associations in the fact that he follows the rivers in his search for her, and particularly in the fact that she is constantly invisible to him. She is thus an image of the denying mother, as is also suggested by the fact that the tritons—dwellers of the sea who naturally need a great deal of liquid—wither at her feet in adoration. This blending of genital and pregenital elements is doubly significant in view of the fact that the serpent woman-phallic mother alone can reveal the presence of the nymph to him.

The description of Lamia is rich in significant details which suggest her as pregenital mother image. She is said to have a gordian shape and thus reminds us of the knot which no one could untie (denying mother) except Alexander who cut it with his sword-phallus. She is striped like a zebra and thus suggests the horse symbol, and freckled like a pard and is thus the devouring cat-mother. The aggressive and masochistic elements are stressed in that she is called a demon's mistress and a penanced lady elf. Like Ariadne, who was abandoned by Theseus, she has a starry crown which is to be related to the silver moons of her skin. Stress is also laid on her peacock eyes that can only weep to symbolize the jealous giving mother, and her mouth which gives forth honeyed words. It is also significant that Hermes hovers over her like a falcon about to take his prey. Nevertheless Lamia relates that Hermes has found it impossible to enjoy the oral pleasures represented by the singing of the Muses and Apollo and has therefore come to Crete—albeit like a Phoebean dart. She also makes Hermes swear by his serpent rod that he will repay her favors, for it is she who has rendered the nymph invisible and thus immune from suitors. The words of this oath are blown among the blossoms to indicate its genital significance, but the pregenital means of attainment is suggested by the fact that the Circean Lamia breathes upon Hermes' eyes-mouth in order to make the nymph appear. The nymph herself at first seems like a moon in wane, that is, denying light, but soon the images change to those of flowers and bees, and Hermes and his lady love steal off to fulfill their doubtful heterosexual destiny.

The change which Lamia now undergoes is truly dreadful. The foam which comes from her mouth is so poisonous that it withers the grass. There are volcanic images which suggest the horror of the breast and which eclipse the milder mooned grace of her body. Finally there is nothing left to her but ugliness and pain and from her lips comes the cry of Lycius to be borne among the mountain mists. (The name of Lycius suggests the archer god Apollo, one of whose epithets may mean wolf-suckled and thus indicate the infant aggressively attached to the breast.) The ambivalence with which she is surrounded is suggested by the fact that in spite of her recent ugliness she now appears as a full blown beauty.[3] Her pregenital character is seen in the fact that she awaits Lycius near a pool-breast about a young bird's flutter from a wood. Finally her attachment to masochistic elements in pregenital experience is indicated by her ability:

> ... *in the lore*
> *Of love deep learned to the red heart's core:*
> *Not one hour old, yet of sciential brain*
> *To unperplex bliss from its neighbor pain;*
> *Define their pettish limits, and estrange*
> *Their points of contact, and swift counterchange:*
> *Intrigue with the specious chaos, and dispart*
> *Its most ambiguous atoms with sure art:*

Keats further describes her by telling of her visits to Thetis, the mother of the homosexual Achilles, Bacchus, the oral god of wine, and Mulciber, the impotent lame god of the forge. Finally he tells how she saw Lycius at a chariot race, whipping aggressively the horse-symbol, at Corinth, the city of courtesans.

The meeting of Lamia and Lycius is also descriptive of the attachment between mother and child on the pregenital level. Lycius has been to sacrifice at the shrine of Jove and this appeal to the paternal principle would seem to bode well for him. But there may be the same sort of irony here as that which makes Zeus appear to patronize Achilles in Homer's *Iliad*. For all Jove's favor, both Lycius and Achilles are destroyed by the breast complex. There is some indication of this in the fact that Lycius is discovered wandering alone over the solitary hills which are familiar breast symbols and in his fantasy "lost in the calmed twilight of Platonic shades"—that is, homosexual love. He is thus indifferent to the first appeal of his future mistress and she accordingly cries to him to look back—a thing forbidden to the worshipers of Hecate on pain of incurring her displeasure. As he does he drinks her beauty as from a bewildering cup and thinks of her as a naiad whom the streams obey.[4] Like the child at the breast he fears that she may vanish and that then he will die or waste to a shade. Lamia, for her part, says that she cannot stay because the flowers with their genital significance are too rough for her finer, Platonic spirit. And as she is about to leave, he swoons to suggest his impotence and his drooping head is only revived by her putting her lips to his. She now adopts different tactics and seems to begin to play the courtesan. She whispers woman's love to him and brings him through the city's gates (feminine genitals) he knows not how, past the lewd temples of Corinth, past the dreaded figure of Lycius' philosopher teacher whose bald head again symbolizes castration and impotence, to her house known only to Persian mutes, her slaves. This change in Lamia from goddess to real woman would seem to indicate a shift from pregenital to genital level, but the clandestine atmosphere which surrounds the change betrays the unstable and defensive character of this relationship. Yet this approach to genital experience is needed in order to maintain even a momentary attachment to Lamia.

But the masochistic character of their love is indicated in the opening lines of Part II where Keats tells us that

> *Love in a hut, with water and a crust,*
> *Is—Love, forgive us!—cinders, ashes, dust;*
> *Love in a palace is perhaps at last*
> *More grievous torment than a hermit's fast:—*
> *That is a doubtful tale from fairy land,*
> *Hard for the non-elect to understand.*

The influence of the breast complex is further suggested by the fact that this same love buzzes with his wings like the bird-breast, making the fearful roar of the devouring mother outside their chamber door. Moreover the first hint of Lycius' destructive attack on the mother image come when he hears a sound of trumpets symbolizing warlike aggression from a neighboring hill-breast. It is so loud that it deafens the swallow's *(n.b.* the oral pun) twitter. The form which his aggression takes, however, is to insist on a public marriage to eradicate the clandestine taint of their love and this marriage he thinks of in terms of a military triumph over his foes. Lamia objects, but Lycius persists and strikes a pose like Apollo about to kill the python and thus symbolizes his aggression against the phallic breast. Lamia, in true masochistic fashion, loves the tyranny and takes luxurious delight in her sorrows.[5] She says, however, that she has no friends, even her parents are dead and forgotten, and she begs Lycius not to invite his teacher Apollonius —whose name derives from the Greek verb meaning to destroy and, of course, from Apollo. So, while she looks upon the whole ceremony as a misery, she sets about preparing her house for the feast. The decorations are a profusion of trees whose phallic stems and arching branches are an ironic comment on the marriage which never takes place.

As the guests arrive they try to recollect from their childhood experience the house to which they are invited. It is significant that they cannot do so. Apollonius arrives, too, uninvited though Lycius is no longer at odds with him as he was at first when he met Lamia. Now he speaks to him with reconciling words which turn into sweet milk the sophist's spleen. Here again, as in *St. Agnes*, Keats uses the description of this feast to suggest the consummation of the lovers' marriage. But it is significant that in the description of this feast, unlike that in *St. Agnes*, there is no mention of solid food, only a description of the furniture and of the drink and the talk. The distribution of the garlands, perhaps a parallel to the symbol of the wedding ring, brings the evening to its climax. Lamia's wreath is made of willow and adder's tongue: grief and the phallic breast, Lycius has one made from thyrsus: the god of wine and oral forgetfulness, and Apollonius one of spear grass: pregenital aggression. Keats takes occasion to point out that natural philosophy will symbolize this aggression as well as anything.

> *Do not all charms fly*
> *At the mere touch of cold philosophy?*
> *There was an awful rainbow once in heaven:*
> *We know her woof, her texture; she is given*
> *In the dull catalogue of common things.*
> *Philosophy will clip an Angel's wings,*
> *Conquer all mysteries by rule and line,*
> *Empty the haunted air, and gnomed mine—*
> *Unweave a rainbow, . . .*

That is to say, such a scientist as Newton has aggressively attacked mother nature by separating her facts from her values. These values, however, are peculiarly masochistic in character. They are the rainbow which is a promise that there will be no more punishing floods from the breast of mother nature, and this rainbow, which is also conceived of as a masochistic denial of voyeuristic sights, is now unwoven. Even the hermaphroditic angels have their wings clipped by science. All this is to be deplored for the masochist loves that sort of mystery wherein aggression and passivity are coexistent. And it now appears that Apollonius and Lycius are but different aspects of the same person. The philosopher is simply a means of shifting the guilt for aggression against the mother image from the hero to a less important character. The effect of the philosopher's steady gaze directed upon Lamia—

eye-mouth aggression against the breast—is first to make her cold and then hot and then speechless. Lycius feels the terror in his hair and tries in vain to control the aggression of the philosopher. Even the threat of conscience does not deter him, for Apollonius' aggression is Lycius' own. Like a sharp spear his gaze continues to make Lamia wither away. This image we shall see Keats applying to his feelings for Fanny Brawne. And although Apollonius tells Lycius that he is doing this to save him from the serpent woman he does not reckon with the masochistic attachment which binds Lycius to Lamia. Thus as the pregenital mother image vanishes with a frightful scream, Lycius himself lies dead upon the couch. The aggression which as Apollonius he turned against Lamia was also directed against himself insofar as he was identified with her.

Some of the significant facts taken from Keats' biography may be noted here. He was born in October 1795, a premature infant of seven months. His mother must have been a very busy woman in the early years of his life. In February 1797 she gave birth to a second son, George; in November 1799 a third, Tom; in April 1801 a fourth, Edward; and in June 1803 a daughter Frances. Sidney Colvin, Keats' biographer, relates the tradition that she is supposed to have hastened the birth of her eldest child by some imprudence. An anecdote given by Haydon illustrates the generally accepted fact that Keats as a child was subject to emotions of considerable violence.

At the age of five years or thereabouts, he once got hold of a naked sword and shutting the door swore nobody should go out. His mother wanted to do so, but he threatened her so furiously she began to cry, and was obliged to wait till somebody through the window saw her position and came to the rescue.

He seems also to have had an infantile trick, when he was first learning to speak, of not answering sensibly but making a rhyme to the last word people said and then laughing. Some rhymes said by Colvin to refer to Keats' reminiscences of the tenth to fifteenth year of his life seem to hark back to this habit. Two of the stanzas are as follows:

There was a naughty boy
    And a naughty boy was he,
For nothing would he do
    But scribble poetry—
        He took
        An ink stand
        In his hand

There was a naughty boy
    And a naughty boy was he
He kept little fishes
    In washing tubs three
        In spite
        Of the might
        Of the Maid

And a pen
Big as ten
In the other,
And away
In a Pother
He ran
To the mountains
And fountains
And ghostes
And Postes
And witches
And ditches
And wrote
In his coat
When the weather
Was cool,
Fear of gout,
And without
When the weather
Was warm—
Och the charm
When we choose
To follow one's nose
To the north,
To the north,
To follow one's nose
To the north!

Nor afraid
Of his Granny-good—
He often would
Hurly burly
Get up early
And go
By hook or crook
To the brook
And bring home
Miller's thumb,
Tittlebat
Not over fat,
Minnows small
As the stall
Of a glove,
Not above
The size
Of a nice
Little Baby's
Little fingers—
O he made
'Twas his trade
Of fish a Pretty Kettle
A Kettle—
A Kettle
Of fish a Pretty Kettle
A Kettle!

If these verses do represent true recollections their symbols will have an obvious meaning which will not need elaboration here. We may note, however, that in addition to these early trials with his mother, the death of his father when he was nine years old and the subsequent unhappy marriage and separation of his mother must have caused him further emotional difficulties.

As a boy Keats was of a pugnacious nature. His brother George said of him in this respect:

From the time we were boys at school, where we loved, jangled, and fought alternately, until we separated in 1818, I in a great measure relieved him by continual sympathy, explanation, and inexhaustible spirits and good humor, from many a bitter fit of hypochondriasm. He avoided teasing anyone with his miseries but Tom and myself, and often asked our forgiveness; venting and discussing them gave him relief.

It is remarkable that this trait, which is attested from several sources disappeared when Keats reached the age of puberty—about fourteen or fifteen.

Previous to this time he had shown little interest in books, but now he became studious. If we assume the existence of a strong masochistic tendencies for which his pugnacity was an appropriate defense, we may see one reason for the abandonment of this defense in the fact that in February 1810 his mother died after a period of illness due to rheumatism and consumption. Unconsciously Keats may have felt her death to have been the climax of his pseudo-aggressive defenses denying his masochistic attachment to her. The defense was abandoned for the more subtle one of study and writing because it was laden with too much guilt. But the new defense expressed in the devouring of books is only another way of saying: I do not want to be denied words-milk, I am not a masochist passively attached to mother, I want to get as much words-milk as I can. So submissive had he become that he apparently offered no opposition to his new guardian's plan to remove him from school and apprentice him to a surgeon. But he evidently had no liking for this profession and soon began to concentrate all his efforts on poetry. There is an anecdote which can be dated at this time which seems to indicate that Keats had substituted writing for fighting.

Keats' relation to women, or rather to the one woman besides his mother with whom he had any intimate relations, is the chief topic of biographical interest in his short adult life. The affair with Fanny Brawne was preluded by the untimely death of his brother Tom in December 1818. In September of that year Keats wrote:

I never was in love, yet the voice and shape of a woman has haunted me these two days—at such a time when the relief of poetry seems a much less crime. This morning poetry has conquered—I have relapsed into those abstractions which are my only life—I feel escaped from a new, strange, and threatening sorrow, and I am thankful for it.

It is possible that the woman here mentioned was Fanny Brawne, and in any case it is probable that he met and fell in love with her soon after this was written. That this love was of a deeply masochistic character, the available evidence seems amply to prove. There are many references in Keats' poetry showing that in his mind love, women, and death were inseparably associated. He seems himself to have been aware of the neurotic character of his attitude toward women. To his friend Bailey he writes:

I am certain I have not a right feeling towards women—at this moment I am striving to be just toward them, but I cannot. Is it because they fall so far beneath my boyish imagination? . . . When I am among men I have no evil thoughts, no malice, no spleen; I feel free to speak or be silent; I can listen, and from everyone I can learn; my hands are in my pockets, I am free from all suspicion, and comfortable. When I am among women, I have evil thoughts, malice, spleen; I cannot speak, or be silent; I am full of suspicions, and therefore listen to nothing; I am in a hurry to be gone . . . I must absolutely get over this—but how?

In a passage to his relatives in America he writes that poetry is his only love:

The roaring of the wind is my wife; and the stars through the window pane are my children . . . According to my state of mind, I am with Achilles shouting in the trenches, or with Theocritus in the vales of Sicily; or throw my whole being into Troilus, and, repeating those lines, "I wander like a lost soul upon the Stygian bank, staying for waftage," I melt into the air with a voluptuousness so delicate, that I am content to be alone.

Some other passages from Keats' letters to Fanny Brawne will substantiate the masochistic character of his attachment. It should not be supposed, however, that the general tone of Keats' letters is typified in these excerpts. I have merely collected the passages relevant to the trait of psychic masochism. In apologizing for his preference of poetry to Fanny he writes to her:

I know the generality of women would hate me for this; that I should have so unsoftened, so hard a mind as to forget them; forget the brightest realities for the dull imaginations of my own brain. But I conjure you to give it a fair thinking; and ask yourself whether 'tis not better to explain my feelings to you, than write artificial passion—besides you would see through it. It would be vain to strive to deceive you! 'Tis harsh, harsh, I know it— My heart seems now made of iron—I could write a proper answer to an invitation to Idalia.
I have been astonished that men could die martyrs for religion—I have shudder'd at it. I shudder no more—I could be martyr'd for my religion— Love is my religion—I could die for that. I could die for you. My creed is love and you are its only tenet. You have ravish'd me away by a power I cannot resist; and yet I could resist till I saw you; and even since I have seen you I have endeavored often "To reason against the reasons of my love." [A quotation from Ford's 'Tis Pity she's a Whore] I can do that no more—the pain would be too great. My love is selfish. I cannot breathe without you.
I should like to cast the die for love or death. I have no patience with anything else—if you ever intend to be cruel to me as you say in jest now but perhaps may be in earnest be so now—and I will—my mind is in a tremble, I cannot tell what I am writing.
I can do nothing, say nothing, think nothing of you but what has its spring in the love which has so long been my pleasure and torment. On the night I was taken ill—when so violent a rush of blood came to my lungs that I

nearly suffocated—I assure you I felt it possible I might not survive, and at that moment thought of nothing but you. When I said to Brown "this is unfortunate" I thought of you.

How have you passed this month? Who have you smiled with? All this may seem savage in me. You do not feel as I do—you do not know what is is to love—one day you may—your time is not come. Ask yourself how many unhappy hours Keats has caused you in loneliness. For myself I have been a martyr the whole time, and for this reason I speak; the confession is forc'd from me by the torture. I appeal to you by the blood of that Christ you believe in: Do not write to me if you have done anything this month which it would have pained me to have seen. You may have altered—if you have not—if you still behave in the dancing rooms and other societies as I have seen you—I do not want to live—if you have done so I wish this coming night may be my last. I cannot live without you, and not only you but *chaste you; virtuous you.* The sun rises and sets, the day passes, and you follow the bent of your inclination to a certain extent—you have no conception of the quantity of miserable feeling that passes through me in a day.—Be serious! Love is not a plaything—

I see you come down in the morning: I see you meet me at the window—I see everything over again eternally that I ever have seen. If I get on the pleasant clue I live in a sort of happy misery, if on the unpleasant 'tis miserable misery.

To be happy with you seems such an impossibility! it requires a luckier star than mine! it will never be! Hamlet's heart was full of such misery as mine is when he said to Ophelia, "Go to a nunnery, go, go!" Indeed I should like to give up the matter at once—I should like to die. I am sickened at the brute world you are smiling with. I hate men and women more. I see nothing but thorns for the future—wherever I may be next winter in Italy or nowhere Brown will be near you with his indecencies—I see no prospect of any rest. Suppose me in Rome—well, I should there see you as in a magic glass going to and from town at all hours,—I wish you could infuse a little confidence in human nature into my heart. I cannot muster any —the world is too brutal for me—I am glad there is such a thing as the grave—I am sure I shall never have any rest till I get there.

That these masochistic torments remained with him to the last may perhaps be seen from an anecdote related by his friend Severn who says that in the first days of their arrival at Rome Keats began reading Alfieri but dropped the book at the words

Misera me! sollievo a me non resta
Altro che'l pianto, ed il pianto è delitto.

The last words express perfectly the unconscious predicament of the psychic masochist. The significance of Keats' attachment to Fanny Brawne is also found in the order of composition of the three poems discussed in the present chapter. *The Eve of St. Agnes* was begun a few months after the first meeting with Fanny. It must therefore be looked upon as a defense against the masochistic relationship which was already in existence with regard to her. It was a way of saying that normal happy love was possible after all. But Keats knew it was an unsuccessful defense and the composition of *La Belle Dame Sans Merci* a few months later gives a truer picture of his unconscious situation. *Lamia,* which followed these two poems, has the honesty to deal directly with the phallic mother on the pregenital level and with amazing intuition places the blame for the aggression, in itself a defense, where it belongs.

V

SHELLEY

Prometheus Unbound

PROMETHEUS *Unbound* is the most complicated of all the poems which we have considered so far. In it Shelley makes use of all three of the major conflict patterns which are to be found in the development of the unconscious mind. The original drama which Shelley used as a base for his own, Aeschylus' Prometheus, was an expression of the positive oedipus complex. In it Prometheus, as the oedipal son, usurps the privileges of the father, is punished, repents and is forgiven. But the normal course of oedipal justice did not appeal to Shelley. His hatred of the father was seemingly much stronger than that of Aeschylus. It demanded the complete overthrow of Jupiter and the concomitant exoneration of Prometheus for this crime against the father. This exoneration is accomplished by overlaying the positive oedipus complex with a negative oedipus complex whereby the son represses his hatred for the father and puts himself in the mother's place in order to demonstrate his love in the most passive manner. But both the positive and negative oedipus complexes are themselves only defenses against the deeper conflict between the son and the mother. This conflict Shelley has also expressed and we shall see that some of the more obscure portions of the drama, particularly those involving the figure of Demogorgon, are explicable in terms of it.

In the first act of the drama Shelley is primarily concerned with the problem of expressing the shift from the positive to the negative oedipus complex. The more basic conflict between mother and son is kept in the background though it is clearly symbolized in the fact that Prometheus hangs bound to an icy precipice: an infant masochistically attached to the denying mother's breast.[1] As he begins to speak he invokes Jupiter as the supreme tyrant who has enslaved mankind, that is, Prometheus himself. He does, however, exempt one being from this tyranny and this being, as we learn from the course of the drama, is Demogorgon who alone has the power to overthrow Jupiter and hence is not subject to him. Since Demogorgon, as we shall also see later, is primarily a pre-oedipal figure, we have here another allusion to the importance of the pre-oedipal conflict as opposed to the more superficial oedipal one. Prometheus continues to speak more particularly of his own sufferings. Mankind have been afflicted with fear and self-contempt for their rebellion, but Prometheus has, he says, conquered these miseries—though there is perhaps an allusion to Milton's *Samson Agonistes* and the castration theme in the phrase "eyeless in hate." But this empire over pain which Prometheus claims as the virtue of self-mastery may also be viewed as a masochistic acceptance of punishment. For he says that his triumph over pain is more glorious than the ill tyranny of Jupiter which he would have to share if he submitted. This latter remark is also a hit at Aeschylus' solution of the positive oedipus complex though it overlooks the point that Jupiter's tyranny consists primarily in punishing the unwarranted rebellion of Prometheus. Viewed in this light Shelley's Prometheus seems to be considerably less master of himself than Aeschuylus', for the latter at least knows when to submit.

Prometheus now appeals to the earth, its mountains and seas—all mother symbols—and the sun, the symbol of the aggressive, pre-oedipal infant, to bear witness to his pain. He describes his tortures in terms which suggest their infantile masochistic origin from the breast complex. The glaciers are spears and thus symbolize aggression at a distance, the chains eat, the torturing eagle breast-bird is a hound *(cf.* those in attendance on Hecate) who poisons the hero. There are earthquake fiends reminiscent of the devouring mother and whirlwinds with hailstorms which suggest frozen milk. Yet Prometheus is willing to bear all this in anticipation of the downfall of Jupiter and his return to the oedipal defense contains elements of the strong hatred of the positive oedipus which demands the overthrow of Jupiter and of the negative oedipus which demands that Jupiter will be brought to kiss the bloody feet, phallic symbols, of the hero. Thus he foreshadows the feminine identification and the spurious homosexuality which will be his ultimate defense. But this first violent fantasy of Jupiter's downfall is too heavily weighted on the positive side and consequently Prometheus immediately disclaims his hatred and suggests that he pities Jupiter who is to be hunted through heaven. This will be done by someone other than Prometheus and then Jupiter's soul will gape like a hell within in imitation of the devouring mother. Prometheus also declares that he wishes to recall his curse against Jupiter, but due to the passive attitude of "self-mastery" which he has now adopted toward him he cannot remember anything so aggressive. The ambivalence of his attitude is plain from the fact that he desires to hear the curse once more instead of letting it rest quietly in oblivion. It is, so to speak, a last chance to be aggressive before complete passivity.

It is significant that Prometheus must now call as witnesses to the curse various elements which symbolize the pre-oedipal conflict with the mother: mountains and springs for the breast, air and whirlwinds for the oral-respiratory organs. By this we can see that most of the aggression utilized in the positive oedipal curse has a pre-oedipal basis. There is a sense in which the curse is really directed against mother and not against father. It is perhaps for this reason that the voice of the springs says that a pilot-son goes insane and dies on the howling sea-mother at the sound of the curse. So too the mountains collapse, the air is riven and the whirlwinds keep silence to represent the denying and devouring mother. It is therefore appropriate that the Earth, Prometheus' mother, should make her appearance at this moment. She too symbolizes Prometheus' pregenital aggression in oral terms and says that the tongueless caverns, hollow heaven—both mouth symbols—and the ocean climbing the land lamented the curse. The enmity which exists between Prometheus and the Earth is immediately apparent for he replies by saying that she scorns him although it is due to his resistance that Jove has not destroyed her. But though he poses as the unrequited defender of the mother against the father on the oedipal level, his real relations with the mother are seen in his recollection of his wanderings with Asia who is to be the good-mother symbol. At one time he drank life from her eyes-breasts but now no longer. He ends his speech with an appeal to his brothers, having wholly despaired of comfort from his mother.

But the brothers dare not speak, Earth says, and she herself continues to refuse the words of the curse saying that Prometheus cannot understand the language of the dead—thus implying that in some sense she is dead to him. Prometheus now begins to feel the masochistic nature of his attachment to the mother image for he says that he is swept away by love in which there is no pleasure. And although the Earth speaks with the voice of the dead, that is, one who has submitted to a higher power, Prometheus cannot hear her voice since he cannot die in this sense, that is, he cannot submit to her consciously. He asks Earth to reveal her identity and she does so in terms which depict her relation to him on the oedipal as opposed to the pre-oedipal level. It is true that much of the imagery of this speech is given in terms of pre-oedipal symbols, for according to her the punishments which Jupiter inflicts for the oedipal crime fall upon Earth as well as upon Prometheus. Thus she says:

> . . . *foodless toads*
> *Within voluptuous chambers panting crawled:*
> *When plague had fallen on man and beast and worm,*
> *And famine; and black blight on herb and tree;*
> *And in the corn, and vines, and meadow grass,*
> *Teemed ineradicable poisonous weeds*
> *Draining their growth; for my wan breast was dry*
> *With grief;*

But in making the father and not the son responsible for this pre-oedipal aggression, Shelley is presumably using the oedipal conflict as a defense against the pre-oedipal which has come a little too near the surface in the preceding speeches. This speech, then, to some extent reconciles Prometheus to his mother, though he realizes that her genital comforts, her flowers and fruits, are not to be his. Again he implores her not to deny him. And she, having temporarily put aside her pre-oedipal role and assumed the oedipal one, can now deny him less absolutely than she did before. She tells him there is a realm of phantoms which he may call upon to repeat the curse, and mentions among others the phantoms of Demogorgon, Jupiter, Typhon, or that of Prometheus himself.

It is significant that Prometheus does not call up his own phantom to repeat the curse though this would seem the most logical course of action if he really wanted to repent of his aggression. Instead he calls upon the phantom of Jupiter and thus signifies that he only desires to shift from the positive to the negative oedipus relation. For by making the father repeat the curse of the son, Prometheus is able to shift the guilt for his own aggression onto the father image. This leaves him in that completely passive position which is characteristic of the negative oedipus relation and prepares the way for the feminine identification with the mother image which is to occur in the last act of the play. There is also a hidden attack on the father image in this shifting of the son's guilt onto the father, but it should be noted that it is not Prometheus' repentance of the curse at this point in the play which brings about the downfall of Jupiter. Quite the contrary, since the phantasm of Jupiter in speaking the curse, now directed at Prometheus himself, foreshadows the punishments which the real Jupiter is to send in the remainder of the act. Furthermore the whole second act is to intervene before the overthrow of Jupiter comes about and then it is Demogorgon for reasons of its own rather than Prometheus who accomplishes it.

At this moment when Prometheus is beginning his change from the positive and masculine character to the negative and feminine character, we have the first appearance of two of the three good-mother images symbolized in the Oceanides. Ione is a form of Io the cow goddess who in Egyptian mythology is Hathor the moon goddess; Panthea is a form of Pandeia the daughter of the son of Saturn and the moon in Shelley's translation of Homer's hymn to the moon. These two, then, with Asia who is still absent are Shelley's version of the triple moon and mother goddess, otherwise known as Luna, Hecate, and Artemis. Shelley is to use them as the favorable side of his ambivalent concept of the mother. As such they are a defense against the bad-mother image already ambiguously represented by Earth and whose archetype is to be Demogorgon. It is appropriate that they should speak at this moment for in accepting the negative oedipus relation Prometheus must play the role of the wife to the approaching phantasm of Jupiter. The previous rejection of the oedipal mother, Earth, and the pitying dread of Ione and Panthea aid this transition. It is noteworthy that this negative father figure should speak of himself as frail and empty, thus distinguishing himself from the positive father image. It is also interesting that Earth says that the mountains, springs and streams—all pregenital images—and even the woods and caves will rejoice to hear the curse, that is, to hear the aggressive son Prometheus cursed instead of cursing. Her reaction thus differs markedly from that of Panthea and Ione who only fear for Prometheus.

The curse which is now finally spoken is typical of a son with a positive oedipus complex directing his aggression against the father image. But we should remember that in the present context it is not being spoken by Prometheus but Jupiter who in using his son's words is reduced in status from father to son. The object of the curse, however, must now be Prometheus himself and he, as we have seen and shall see more conclusively presently, is on the way toward identifying himself with the mother in the negative oedipus relation. If the curse is read carefully it will be seen that there is nothing in it which will definitely determine the sex of the person against whom it is directed. It can therefore just as well be read as an attack of the preoedipal or negative oedipal son on the mother image or as an attack of the positive oedipal son on the father. It is indeed so ambiguous that its imagery lends support to all three relations. That of the first stanza is primarily a pre-oedipal attack on the mother with emphasis on aggression at a distance, that of the second a positive oedipal attack on the father with emphasis on the erect phallus, that of the third and fourth a negative oedipal attack on the mother with emphasis on passivity and self-torture. At any rate, whoever is the object of this complicated aggression, Prometheus himself now abdicates all responsibility for being its agent. He thus places himself at the mercy of the oedipal father and the pre-oedipal mother whom he has wronged without repenting of his crimes in the way that Aeschylus' Prometheus did. The Earth stresses the calamity of this new passivity of Prometheus by echoing and re-echoing that he lies fallen and vanquished— in a quite different sense from that in which the positive oedipal son is vanquished. Here the Earth speaks in her character as oedipal mother who sees not only the overthrow of the son by the father but also the rejection of the mother by the son.

Ione, however, who may represent the feminine mother identification which Prometheus is now undergoing, does not see things in so gloomy a light. She says that Prometheus is not wholly vanquished and she describes the approach of Mercury, a god whose serpent-cinctured wand often betokens an approaching struggle with the pre-oedipal phallic mother. With him he brings a crowd of furies who may be construed as pre-oedipal mother images out to punish Prometheus for the defensive aggression which is partly responsible for his difficulties. The fact that they are sent by Jupiter, however, is directly related to Prometheus' newly accepted passivity toward the father image. Their coming is thus an expression of masochistic attachment to the father image in accordance with the negative oedipal relation. The fact that these furies have nothing to do with the positive oedipal relation is made clear by Mercury who in trying to restrain them says that he may have them replaced by other fiends, particularly the Sphinx whose connection with the positive oedipal relation is well known. However, he allows the present furies to stay and instead apologizes profusely to Prometheus for the dirty work which he must do. This apology may perhaps be construed as an indication of the fact that the tortures which are to follow are largely self-inflicted. Mercury may actually be more embarrassed by Prometheus' stubborn masochism than by Jupiter's injustice. The way of escape is certainly open for Prometheus and although he says that he cannot take it because it would mean betrayal of mankind yet there are some inconsistencies in his argument. If Jupiter's downfall is really inevitable, as Prometheus says, then Prometheus' prophecies will not affect it and his suffering is needless. Furthermore he says he does not know the exact time of the overthrow and thus his incomplete information might well be useless to Jupiter.

We are thus led to suspect that the ascription of the forthcoming punishment to Jupiter is but a projection of Prometheus' own repressed aggression against the father image. This view is strengthened by the fact that Prometheus in his reply to Mercury insists that he gave Jupiter all he has and therefore cannot submit to him. If we are to take him literally here we must assume that Prometheus is admitting his own masochistic attachment to Jupiter, for he says that Jupiter is merely a puppet of his creation and hence he is being tortured by his own puppet. To put the point in technical terms we might think of Jupiter as the unconscious Super-Ego created by the Ego-Prometheus. To this Super-Ego the Ego submits for purposes of masochistic pleasure although clinical evidence shows that there are masochistic and self-punitive tendencies in the Ego before the formation of the oedipal Super-Ego. In any case Prometheus is determined to enjoy the pain which has been prepared for him. The curtain is run up on the torture scene by a thunderbolt which consumes a snow-laden cedar: symbol of aggression against the denying mother. As the furies come Prometheus in true masochistic fashion says:

> Methinks I grow like what I contemplate
> And laugh and stare in loathsome sympathy.

The furies, however, picture themselves as dogs pursuing a wounded fawn and thus are like the ravenous child attacking the breast, or as roses which lose their color when plucked, suggesting castration or feminine identification as a result of masochistic attachment to the mother image. This latter figure symbolizes the identity between punisher and punished, for the color of the rose is said to fall upon the priestess's cheek as the furies take their shape from whatever they attack.

Prometheus now asks for the cup of pain and says that pain is his element. He further explicitly declares that he is the king who rules these inner torments, and thus must sanction them, as Jove rules Hell. The Chorus of Furies knows this well enough and they cry to each other to leave their former occupation and approach richer fields.

> Leave the self-contempt implanted
> In young spirits, sense-enchanted,
> Misery's yet unkindled fuel:
> Leave Hell's secrets half unchanted,
> To the maniac dreamer; cruel

More than ye can be with hate
Is he with fear!

It is thus clear that Prometheus is his own torturer. The lyrical choruses summon the furies to the masochistic orgy which is to be symbolized in two emblems. The first of these is the crucifixion which is revealed by the rending of the veil of the temple at Jerusalem which is the obstacle to the voyeuristic infant's desire for forbidden sights-milk. Prometheus is further tantalized by having it pointed out to him that the thirst for knowledge which he gave men is an insatiable one. Christ is then shown smiling on the sanguine earth-mother. But His words turn to poison and cities go up in smoke —i.e., vomit—in his wake. The oral background of these images is apparent. The other emblem is that of the French revolution which though based on fraternity ends in mutual murder—masochism and homosexuality. Here again the oral metaphor appears in the comparison of blood to wine. All the furies except one now vanish in order to show that Prometheus is beginning to take over his own torture. Panthea and Ione, who we remember represent his passive identification with the negative oedipal mother figure, see the crucified Christ but are helpless to minister to him and remark that men, like infants at the breast, may be killed with frowns and smiles.

The fury who is left to represent Prometheus' torturing-mother image now says that those who endure wrongs for mankind only heap more wrongs on themselves, that is, they are unconscious masochists. Prometheus tacitly agrees, for speaking to the image of the crucified Christ he counsels Him not to struggle any longer but seek peace in death—the ultimate masochistic solution. He now becomes subject to a phantasmagoria of delusions of persecution and the fury takes up the tale to show in how many ways men have contrived to torture themselves. She ends with an echo of the words of Christ on the cross: "They know not what they do." Here again we see how the fury, the torturing-mother image, is but a projection of the sufferer's own masochistic tendencies. Prometheus speaks of her words as winged snakes symbolic of the phallic breast and shows his complete submersion in the masochistic orgy by saying that he pities those who are not tortured by them. The fury upon hearing this departs for she sees that her presence is no longer needed. Prometheus will now torture himself unaided. Still he says that he will not seek refuge in death, as he advised the image of Christ on the cross, and thus indicates that there is still some hope for a defense against the basic masochistic conflict. He also relates to Panthea the meaning of the emblem of the French revolution, suggesting that the revolutionists were betrayed by the fickle goddess of reason whom they worshiped. It is certainly true that the masochistic conflicts throughout this scene have been with the mother images rather than the father image, though the latter is supposed to be ultimately responsible.

Earth now speaks and says with malicious ambiguity that she has felt Prometheus'

> *tortures with such mixed joy*
> *As pain and virtue give.*

It is thus not clear whether she is gloating or sympathizing, though she is now willing to cheer him with certain spirits who foresee Prometheus' future. These spirits do prophesy the unbinding of Prometheus from his masochistic attachment to his breast-precipice, but their character is otherwise not reassuring. They are described as birds in the wind, fountain vapors and fish in the wave, all of which symbols suggest the oral masochistic attachment to the breast. The first spirit is evidently a battle spirit and speaks hopefully of the triumph of love over aggression. But the allusion to the tyrant's banner suggesting rebellion against the oedipal father seems to preclude a normal heterosexual sort of love. The second spirit is a storm spirit who after witnessing a shipwreck sees a man masochistically resign his plank-phallus to his enemy. Here the homosexual overtones grow stronger. The third is a spirit of knowledge who sees a sage fall asleep while "feeding" on his book-breast and then plagued by a dream which will bring him great sorrow. The fourth is the spirit of poetry who tells of a poet watching bees in the ivy bloom suggestive of heterosexuality which he nevertheless does not heed or see except to create poetry from them. The rejection of heterosexuality is here again apparent.

Ione now speaks and says she beholds two more spirits approach in the shape of doves—breast symbols. These two spirits reiterate the masochistic nature of love though much more explicitly. The fifth sees Love scattering liquid joy, milk from the breast, but Ruin yawns behind as devouring mother. In calling Prometheus the king of sadness, however, we are reminded of his negative oedipal character. The sixth spirit deliberately calls Love a monster in whose shadow is desolation and pain. The first chorus of these spirits again stresses the rejection of heterosexuality symbolized by Ruin astride Death which tramples down flowers and weeds. Prometheus however is to destroy this horseman and with him the possibility of heterosexual, oedipal, conflict. The second chorus says that the time for this is the coming of spring when the snowstorms flee the red buds, that is, when the denying mother becomes more auspicious as she will in the person of Asia in

Act II. And certainly a change has now come over Prometheus. He thinks
of Asia and the time when his being overflowed and she was like a chalice
to him. This at first seems like a heterosexual image, but Prometheus adds
that had Asia not been there, the thirsty earth would have drunk up the
liquid. Prometheus has here simply reversed the pre-oedipal child-mother
roles. The thirsty child is now the giving mother and the mother is the
thirsty one, except that she is maliciously denied by having the chalice of
Asia interposed. This would seem to point to Asia as a pre-oedipal mother
image. In any case Prometheus sums up his present situation by saying that
Earth, the bad pre-oedipal mother, can no longer console him; and Heaven,
Jupiter as oedipal father, can no longer torment him.

If Asia is the good pre-oedipal mother-wife image, we may look upon
her separation from Prometheus as due to the necessity he was under of
playing the role of rebellious son in the positive oedipal relation. As soon
as he abandons this role and takes up the negative attitude she can leave
her icy vale which, in turn, may symbolize her connection with the pre-
oedipal denying mother in the mind of Prometheus while he was bound to
the precipice-breast. The fact that her valley is in India may point to the
same connection since the geographical shape of India is that of a breast attached to the continent of Asia. Her awakening with the coming of spring
may also indicate a transition from the wintry denying mother-earth image
on the pre-oedipal level to a more gracious pre-oedipal mother-wife with
whom Prometheus is to identify—or more precisely, whom he is to use as a
defense against his masochistic attachments to the pre-oedipal mother symbolized as Earth, the Furies, Demogorgon and to the oedipal father symbolized by Jupiter. The coming of Panthea to Asia thus establishes the connection between Prometheus and this new mother image. Panthea excuses
the delay in her arrival by saying that she was disturbed by a dream about
Prometheus the gist of which is that his wound-worn limbs fall from him
and his body grows radiant with glory. Love streams from him and his presence flows through Panthea's body and from hers into Ione's. The meaning
of the dream is evidently that Prometheus throws off his character as rebellious oedipal son and assumes the negative oedipal attitude, identifying with
the good, hence giving, pre-oedipal mother as well. Thus Prometheus defends himself against the pre-oedipal mother as well as the oedipal father.
The fact is further stressed by Asia seeing in Panthea's eyes-breasts the
image of Prometheus like the moon giving forth its radiance.

But at this point another dream of Panthea's interposes between Asia
and her vision of Prometheus. It is that of an almond tree which bursts in-

to blossom suggestive of heterosexuality but which is immediately withered by a cold wind to indicate regression to the pre-genital level. On the leaves of this tree are stamped the grievous words, "Follow" "Follow," which are to lead to the cave of Demogorgon, the archetype of the pre-oedipal phallic mother and the negative oedipal father (insofar as he is to replace Jupiter) combined. Asia has had a dream in which these same words were found in the shadows of clouds over the mountain-breasts, on the herbs from which the dew-milk had fallen, whispered by the wind among the pines as phallic breasts and in Panthea's eyes. The very crags, reminiscent of Prometheus' precipice, mock these words with wild echoes which are like dew stars. They are invited to go where the wild bee, the messenger of heterosexuality, never flew, into a world where sleeps a voice unspoken, that of the denying mother, to a world where are the chasms of the devouring mother, where Earth reposed from spasms brought about by the separation of Asia and Prometheus by pre-oedipal aggression. The journey which Asia and Panthea are about to make is a regression back through the genital level of experience to the pregenital level where alone the fate of Prometheus can be discovered.

In accordance with this, Scene II of the act is a forest with rocks and caverns which symbolize the male and female genitals. Asia and Panthea pass through this forest and after they are gone a semichorus of Spirits is heard. They describe the forest as impenetrable to the pregenital symbols of sun, moon, wind, and rain. Flowers are said to be dew hung by mist and star beams sometimes find a cleft to penetrate. In the second semichorus we are already receding from the genital level for the nightingales therein described are symbols of the breast conflict through the myth of Philomela. Some stress is still laid on the love between mates and the blossom from which they sing their laments. The next semichorus recedes still further from the genital level for here we are already under the influence of Demogorgon whose irresistible power draws all towards the fatal peak of the phallic breast. The two fauns who have been sitting by listening now tell us something about the spirits we have just heard. Some are said to be housed in bubbles-breasts which the sun sucks from flowers at their heterosexual birth at the bottom of lakes. Others are said to live in flowers and are thus wholly on the genital level. The spirits then are personifications of the various levels of sexuality as we have already seen from their lyrics. The second faun concludes the scene with a reference to the milking of Silenus' goats and the story of the brotherhood which Prometheus will establish on earth and which will silence the complaining nightingales. It thus appears that some sort of homosexuality is to be a defense against the masochistic attachment to the breast.

In the third scene Asia and Panthea have arrived on a pinnacle of rock among the mountains of Demogorgon's realm—an appropriate landscape for the pregenital level of experience. Panthea speaks of the volcano-like portal as a fountain from which men drink the maddening wine of life.

> *Hither the sound has borne us—to the realm*
> *Of Demogorgon, and the mighty portal,*
> *Like a volcano's meteor-breathing chasm,*
> *Whence the oracular vapor is hurled up*
> *Which lonely men drink wandering in their youth,*
> *And call truth, virtue, love, genius, or joy,*
> *That maddening wine of life, whose dregs they drain*
> *To deep intoxication;*

Asia gives a more panoramic description, noting the forests and caves of the genital level through which they have passed and which lie far below in the mist. Far above are snow-capped peaks of the pregenital denying mother. The sound of cataracts and avalanches shake the mountain-breasts and thus symbolize Prometheus' new defense of the giving mother personified in Asia. Panthea has visions of foodless men like starving infants at the breast wrecked on some oozy isle and Asia sees the shapes of spirits who sing the lyric which concludes the scene. In these stanzas we get a glimpse of the double nature of Demogorgon who as we have already noted is both pre-oedipal phallic mother and negative oedipal father image. It is in the latter character that he is needed to replace the positive oedipal Jupiter. The dual sex of Demogorgon may have been suggested by Boccaccio's picture of him and his spouse Eternity. Shelley combines wife and husband into one figure similar to Boccaccio's description of Eternity as an aged woman encircled by a snake, that is, the phallic mother.[2]

In the first stanza the spirit tells us that in going down into the deepest, earliest level of human experience we must pass through the strife of death and life, Eros and Thanatos and through the veil and bar of the denying mother. The second stanza states a number of breast conflict images: fawn and hound, lightning and vapor, moth and taper, steel and lodestone. In each case the first term symbolizes the aggressive infant, the second the breast. In these stanzas, then, the stress is on the phallic mother. The third stanza shows a transition to the genital level of the negative oedipal father as symbolized by the erasing of the pregenital moon-star symbol and the yoking of the womb-breast symbol in cavern-crag. In the fourth stanza the diamond in the mine suggests the genital level alone and in the fifth we have a combination of the two. For the spirits counsel Asia and through her Prometheus not to resist the weakness and meekness which is characteristic of the passive relation of the son toward the father in the negative oedipal situation. It is only when Prometheus plays the role of wife and mother to Demogorgon that he can unloose the snakelike doom of the phallic breast and bring about the pseudo-homosexual relationship which is his goal. For a genuine homosexual relationship does not involve the negative oedipus relation but is based solely on a pre-oedipal conflict. It is this spurious homosexuality, which was characteristic of Shelley himself, that is to serve as the defense against the masochistic conflicts with pre-oedipal mother and negative oedipal father. Each way Prometheus, and Shelley, is accepting the guilt for the lesser crime, that is the aggression of spurious homosexuality as opposed to the passivity of masochism. Here Demogorgon appears in his role as negative oedipal father; in the fourth act we shall see her as pre-oedipal mother. In both instances heterosexuality is rejected because the major crime of masochistic attachment is only repressed and not overcome.

In the fourth scene Panthea and Asia approach the throne of Demogorgon which is situated in a cave within the peak to symbolize the dual nature of this ultimate being—pregenital and genital, breast and womb. The questions which Asia now directs at Demogorgon are intended to discover who is the source of evil in Prometheus' world and hence with whom his deepest conflict is. She first asks who made the living world, the powers of mind and the ecstasy of young love? Demogorgon ambiguously replies that it is God, but when Asia later asks who is this God, Demogorgon replies that it is Jove whom he did not name directly out of courtesy for Asia's sympathy with Prometheus. Shelley thus has the honesty to realize that Jupiter, who as the representative of the familial and heterosexual principle of things, must also be recognized as the creative principle of things even though Shelley can find no room in his own psychic world for this normal and heterosexual familial principle. Asia comes to the point, however, in asking next who made the various forms of evil. Demogorgon now no longer replies God, but speaks even more obscurely saying: "He reigns." In the long speech which Asia makes describing the role which Prometheus had in the history of mankind, we discover toward the end that she is sure that Jupiter is not the ultimate source of evil. He is only a slave to evil and thus not evil itself. Demogorgon agrees with her in this but is reluctant to name the real source still—and this is typical of a denying-mother image. Nevertheless Demogorgon suggests that the answer might be found by looking on the revolving world, that is, Earth as mother, and by speaking of Fate,

Time, etc. Now since Demogorgon is Fate it is plain that he, or she, is referring to himself as the source of evil in his capacity of pre-oedipal mother principle. In this scene Shelley may have in mind Spenser's Agapé who visits the house of Demogorgon and obtains from the three fatal sisters there a reprieve from death for her sons. In Spenser the mother principle is plainly dominant and Shelley's adoption of this idea is unavoidable since he is presently to make Demogorgon bring about the overthrow of Jupiter.

If Demogorgon is speaking of himself as the ultimate source of evil in his capacity as pre-oedipal mother we can now understand why Asia should interpose her long and slightly irrelevant speech in defense of Prometheus at this point. For the pre-oedipal mother image is only the source of evil to the infant who is masochistically attached to her and since this is the case with Prometheus, the guilt actually lies with him and not with any external source of evil. The realization of this fact makes Asia, his feminine identification as wife, spring to his defense with the speech proving that he has been the benefactor of mankind and not a self-torturer. It is noteworthy, however, that while some of the imagery describing Prometheus' benefactions is drawn from the genital level (in accordance with the Aeschylean story of Prometheus as an oedipal son), most of it has to do with the pregenital, oral level of experience. The speech, then, is calculated to refute the masochistic attachment to pre-oedipal mother and negative oedipal father by saying: "I do not want to be refused by her, I give;" and, "I do not want to be overwhelmed by him, I create." Nevertheless, immediately following her long speech, Asia gets the answer from Demogorgon which we have already noted: that is, that Demogorgon himself is the ultimate cause of evil. The importance of this knowledge for Prometheus and his alter ego Asia is that it shows them what steps must be taken in order to defend themselves from the masochistic attachment to the breast symbolized by the rock to which Prometheus is bound: that is, Prometheus and Asia must adopt the attitude of the giving as opposed to the denying mother. We have already had several indications that this is taking place. More are to follow before Prometheus is finally unbound.

The answers of Demogorgon have now prepared Asia to ask when Prometheus will be freed and Demogorgon answers by pointing to the chariots of the hours which are ready to overthrow Jupiter and free Prometheus. The meaning of these symbolic Hours seems to be that Prometheus is to be freed and Jupiter overthrown by some form of pregenital aggression: Time as a stream. The Hours do not ride on the horses in heterosexual fashion, but drive them furiously from their chariots, perhaps symbolic of the womb. The charioteers themselves are pursued by fiends in the shape of stars, pregenital infants, and their oral character is seen in their eager desire to drink the wind of their own speed. Demogorgon now mounts one of these chariots in the form of darkness and shadow, and Asia and Panthea another which is like a shell and which has a charioteer with dovelike eyes. The lyric which this charioteer speaks stresses the oral traits of his steeds and their aggressive speed. In Scene V their chariot pauses on a snowy peak symbolic of the denying breast where Asia is to experience the irradiating effluence which is to be one of the prime causes in the unloosing of Prometheus. His conflict with the pregenital mother image is based on his passive wish to be refused. Asia's wish to give is to be his defense against this masochistic attachment. But the sort of giving which Asia represents is only defensive and does not indicate a normal heterosexual adjustment. For the spirit at the opening of the scene says that Earth has whispered a warning that their flight must be swifter than fire, that is, that their aggression against the mother image must be hypernormal.

That there is a hidden destructiveness in Asia's radiance appears from the fact that Panthea can scarcely support its brilliance. She compares Asia's present change with her birth as Aphrodite and we remember that the myth tells us that Aphrodite was born from the castrated genitals of Chronos when Zeus overthrew him. The negative oedipal relation may therefore be lurking in the background. Asia now speaks of the power of love, that it makes the reptile, phallic breast, equal to the god and that it makes those most happy who have suffered long. She adds "as I shall soon become" and thus implies that her union with Prometheus will simply mean their identification. A voice in the air now sings about Asia's illumination and makes explicit the association: light-knowledge-words-milk-liquid. It is true that the stanzas are not as clearly stated as they might be. But their general drift is clear.

> Fair are others; none beholds thee,
>   But thy voice sounds low and tender
> Like the fairest, for it folds thee
>   From the sight, that liquid splendor,
> And all feel, yet see thee never,
> As I feel now, lost forever!
>
> Lamp of Earth! where'er thou movest
> Its dim shapes are clad with brightness,
> And the souls of whom thou lovest

Walk upon the winds with lightness,
Till they fail, as I am failing,
Dizzy, lost, yet unbewailing!

He thus stresses the fact that this illumination contains a hidden power of destruction. This once more makes apparent the defensive nature of Asia's giving attitude. And she now sings a lyric of her own which describes the course of her enchanted boat between mountains and woods, that is, between the pre-oedipal and oedipal conflict, into a sea which seems to be the passive effeminacy of the negative oedipal relation. For in the second stanza the music is said to harmonize heaven and earth, male and female, though this is clearly not a normal heterosexual level for the imagery is predominately oral. The last stanza stresses the regressive nature of the voyage and the goal with its vaulted bowers, downward-gazing flowers, and watery paths suggest the combination of hetero- and homosexuality which is characteristic of the negative oedipus relation. Here, too, the shapes are too bright to see and are thus defensively hyperaggressive.

It is significant that immediately following the establishment of Asia's defense against the pre-oedipal denying mother, Shelley should give us the scene in which the downfall of Jupiter is accomplished. For this defense against the denying mother also makes possible the feminine identification of the negative oedipal relation and this in turn serves as a defense against the positive oedipal relation and makes possible its destruction, that is, its repression. Jove, on the other hand, in the opening speech of the scene seems to know well enough that the opposition to his rule stems from pregenital aggression against the mother image. His curses fall like snow on herbless peaks-breasts, but these earliest tendencies nevertheless remain unrepressed. Indeed his weakness is foreshadowed in the boast which he makes concerning the birth of the son in whom he places all his hopes. He quotes Thetis, his wife, as saying that his approach to her made her feel "like *him* whom the Numidian seps did thaw into a dew." This may mean that between Jupiter and Thetis there already exists a negative oedipal relation for she seems to have both feminine and masculine traits. More important, however, is the fact that it is Demogorgon who overthrows Jupiter. He is called the child of Jupiter insofar as the positive oedipal relation, symbolized by Jupiter himself, precedes and gives birth to the negative oedipal relation. So the positive oedipal relation is now repressed by the negative one and this is symbolized by the two falling into the abyss like vulture, pregenital breast, and snake, to symbolize the homosexual component of the negative oedipal relation. The ease with which this overthrow comes about, however, may mean that the positive oedipal relation is only repressed and not destroyed by the negative relation. Moreover both these oedipal patterns are only defenses against the deeper conflict with the pre-oedipal mother which remains unsolved, as we shall see in Act IV. Her part in the overthrow of the positive oedipal relation must be viewed as a triumph of pre-oedipal regression, using the spurious homosexuality of the negative oedipal relation as a defense against the more basic conflict.

The second scene of the act is almost as important as the first. For just as that symbolizes the repression of the positive oedipal relation, so this symbolizes the pacification, if only temporarily, of the pre-oedipal mother image on whom the infant at the breast projects its own ravenous desires. In order to dramatize this aspect of the action Shelley introduces two new characters. The first is Ocean, the father of the Oceanides Panthea, Asia, and Ione, reclining at the mouth of a river which symbolizes the giving breast. The second is Apollo, symbol of infantile aggression at a distance. Apollo relates the fall of Jupiter to a well-pleased Ocean who says that now his streams will flow unstained by the blood of oedipal conflicts. The negative oedipal solution is again hinted at in the image of the inverted flowers reflected in the waves. Peace has been established because Prometheus is now defended against the pre-oedipal mother and oedipal father. Pacification of the pre-oedipal mothers appears from the fact that Ocean says he must go to feed the loud deep which is hungering for calm. The Nereids, too, are weaving sea-flower crowns for their sister Asia, though sea flowers do not seem to be a particularly healthy type of flora.

In the third scene of the act Prometheus is finally unbound, but Shelley does not make much of the unbinding itself since the external act is unimportant compared to the inner consequence. He uses a new and unfamiliar character to accomplish it and we hear nothing of this Hercules afterwards. And Prometheus after thanking Hercules more for his gentle words than for his deed turns to Asia. Their reunion is more like that of brother and sister than lover and beloved. Prometheus begins to describe the ambiguous heterosexual-homosexual paradise which they are to enjoy. The cave itself suggests the genital level, but its fountains and frozen stalactites suggest the pregenital level. It is certainly not an ideal adjustment for masochism still forces the ladies to sigh and Prometheus to smile at them or vice versa. Toward the end of the speech we see that the natural purpose of heterosexuality has been abandoned for the offspring which this union produces are not real children but the sublimated creations of art.

The reason why Prometheus' picture of his future happiness seems unsatisfactory is his unsolved conflict with the mother image. The attempt to solve this conflict is to occupy the rest of the play. Prometheus' first attempt in this direction is to give the spirit of the hour a shell through which he is to pour harmonious sounds upon the unregenerate earth-mother. The shell, a pun on the poet's name, is perhaps a symbol for the ear and mouth, both of which are receiving organs through the latter is turned into a giving organ by the oral regressive in his attempt to refute the pre-oedipal mother image. The aggressive character of this spirit of the hour is emphasized by Prometheus when he tells him to outspeed the sun who, as we have seen, is a type of pregenital infantile aggression. At this point Prometheus appeals directly to the Earth herself who cuts him short by saying that she feels his lips giving warmth to her withered bosom—thus reversing the infantile situation where the mother is the giver. She expresses the change which is now coming over the world in typically oral terms.

> . . . all plants,
> And creeping forms, and insects rainbow-winged,
> And birds and beasts, and fish, and human shapes,
> Which drew disease and pain from my wan bosom,
> Draining the poison of despair, shall take
> And interchange sweet nutriment; to me
> Shall they become like sister-antelopes
> By one fair dam, snow-white and swift as wind,
> Nursed among lilies near a brimming stream.

But though Earth admits that Prometheus is accomplishing a transformation in her supposedly bad character, she cannot help mentioning a fly in the ointment, namely death. Mother, as Prometheus wants her, still has death in her power and Asia reproaches her as a killjoy for mentioning it. But Earth, whose character as bad mother is really not affected by Prometheus' defensive demonstrations, insists on discussing it.

Nevertheless she moderates her harshness when she begins to describe the cave reserved for Prometheus and Asia. Her description, too, hovers between the heterosexual and homosexual level. Moreover, Earth herself now makes the first substantial move toward making possible the goal which Shelley has set for Prometheus. She calls up the spirit of a winged child, her torch bearer as Prometheus is, who is to lead the lovers to their cave. This spirit is obviously the regressive and infantile form of Prometheus himself and furthermore he is the transition stage in Prometheus' metamorphosis into the feminine identification with the mother image, Earth, in Act IV. This is to be his final defense against the oedipal and pre-oedipal conflicts.

It is significant that it is Earth alone who has the power to call up this infantile form of Prometheus, for the latter's masochistic attachment to the mother image renders him helpless to accomplish anything but defensive aggressive measures against her. Earth characterizes this masochistic attachment by saying that the Spirit let his lamp go out by gazing on her eyes, that is, by ravenous desires for the breast which make him think of it as denying. But he kindled it anew, aggressively, from those same eyes. This is, as we have seen, precisely the pattern of Prometheus' experience.

In the concluding scene of the third act we have the arrival of Prometheus and his party at their destined cave. It is significant, however, that Prometheus himself plays little or no part in this scene, although the Spirit of the Earth into whom he is being metamorphosed plays an important part. Panthea and Ione confirm this view by telling us something of the Spirit's pre-Jovian experiences with Asia when the Spirit called her mother.

> . . . *Before Jove reigned*
> *It loved our sister Asia, and it came*
> *Each leisure hour to drink the liquid light*
> *Out of her eyes, for which it said it thirsted*
> *As one bit by a dipsas. . . .*

No mention is made of Prometheus as father and hence we have further proof for the view that Asia and Prometheus are mother and son as well as husband and wife. The Spirit relates to its mother Asia the changes which have been coming over Earth-mother as a result of Prometheus' sending forth the Spirit of the Hour. The results, however, are again slightly ambiguous. Things are only "somewhat changed." There is a suspicious preoccupation with the beauty of snakes, symbolizing the phallic breast, and the final image is of two halcyons clinging downward to a drooping bough, suggesting the inverted sexuality which is Prometheus' goal. Asia now says that the Spirit and she will never part until the Spirit's chaste sister the moon becomes warm. She thus points ahead to Act IV where Prometheus is to become, unambiguously, the Earth-mother in masculine form, and Asia his sister the moon. The spirit of the Earth confirms this relation by saying that then the moon will love Earth as Asia now loves Prometheus. We also learn why the drama cannot be concluded with Act III. It is because Prometheus is not yet wholly metamorphosed into his mother identification and because Asia, as moon-mother, is still cold and denying. This change can only be achieved lyrically in Act IV. The concluding speech of the scene which is a description of the change wrought in Earth by the Spirit of the Hour is chiefly devoted to attacking the oedipal father principle which is now presumably overthrown. The deeper conflict with the mother, however, still remains a source of evil and the final lines of the act refer to it as the clogs which restrain the infant-star who else might be pinnacled, at the breast, dim in the intense inane—the emptiness of the denying-mother image!

Although at the close of Act III the Spirit of the Hour had described the immobilization of his aggressive chariot, we cannot evidently take this literally for in the opening of Act IV the sun as infantile aggression has driven all the stars from heaven like fawns fleeing a leopard-mother. This hints at the fact that the tension between child and mother is never to be wholly resolved. A train of dark forms appears who weep the fall of the father principle and strew hair as a castration symbol on his pall. Panthea and Ione awaken and remark that Jupiter was overthrown by one who foiled his conquest. Various choruses of Spirits and Hours sing lyrics which prelude the coming of some diviner day of joy and triumph, although it is not easy to tell from them just what the character of the triumph is to be. This appears more clearly from the conversation of Panthea and Ione which follows. They see two visions the first of which is emblematic of Asia as Spirit of the Moon being metamorphosed into the Moon and the second of which is Prometheus as Spirit of the Earth metamorphosed into the Earth. (The quaint conception of a child within a globe may be traceable to the illustration for Emblem VI, Book V, of Francis Quarles' poetic emblems.) The poem attached to this emblem has to do with the rejection of Earth for a heavenly father.) But the important point in each of these descriptions is that the child within each of these spheres-breasts is highly aggressive, although more space is devoted to the power inherent in the Spirit of the Earth than in the Spirit of the Moon.

Now follows the ecstatic dialogue between the Earth and Moon during the course of which the moon loses her coldness toward her son the earth and the earth by giving his heat to the moon thus frees himself from the guilt of having attacked her. The earth, brother and son of the moon-mother, is primarily concerned to put the guilt of oral frustration on her.

> *How art thou sunk, withdrawn, covered, drunk up*
> *By thirsty nothing, as the brackish cup*
> *Drained by a desert troop, a little drop for all. . . .*

The sister-moon, on the other hand, replies:

> *The snow upon my lifeless mountains*
> *Is loosened into living fountains,*
> *My solid oceans flow, and sing, and shine:*

> *A spirit from my heart bursts forth,*
> *It clothes with unexpected birth*
> *My cold bare bosom. Oh! it must be thine*
> *On mine, on mine!*

In his second group of lyrics the earth vents his malice on the fallen positive oedipal principle whose father image is now the sun, around whom both earth and moon revolve. It is now clear why Shelley made Apollo the narrator of Jupiter's fall in the scene where he speaks to Ocean. But man, whose incomplete transformation we have already noted in Act III, is now to be left to cure himself. This he will do in typically oral fashion.

> *Leave man, even as a leprous child is left,*
> *Who follows a sick beast to some warm cleft*
> *Of rocks, through which the might of healing springs is poured;*
> *Then when it wanders home with rosy smile,*
> *Unconscious, and its mother fears awhile*
> *It is a spirit, then, weeps on her child restored.*

The moon ends her part of the dialogue with a frenzied lyric in which she characterizes herself as an insatiate bride drinking from the weird cup of Agave—the Earth. Earth replies by saying that her light soothes him as it does the seaman with tiger joy. It is evident that we have arrived at a none-too-stable solution and consequently Demogorgon, as the image of the pre-oedipal phallic mother and the negative oedipal father, now appears to invoke earth, moon, and the other elements who represent Shelley's conception of mankind.

His final word, significantly, is directed against the oedipal and genital level of experience, for he, or she, says that if the serpent-phallus which is now confined to the pit should ever be permitted by the mother image, Eternity, to clasp her waist, then only certain spells with a very strong taint of masochism (endless suffering and endurance) will be sufficient to re-establish the pregenital and negative oedipal situation which Shelley found the ultimate fate in his own life. The final result of the complicated action of this great poem is to permit the Promethean Shelley to accept the guilt for the lesser crime of the negative oedipus relation and escape that of two greater crimes—masochistic attachment to the pregenital mother and rebellion against the positive oedipal father. It is also a way of allowing him to eat his cake and have it too, for he is permitted to employ the defensive trait of spurious homosexuality which says: I reject mother, not she me, in order to escape the guilt of masochism without ever incurring guilt of true homosexuality. It is perhaps for this latter reason that Shelley's personal effeminacy could be so obvious without causing him greater embarrassment than it did.

Anecdotes of Shelley's childhood are just as scarce as in the case of any of the other Romantic poets. He was a first child, born on August 4, 1792. His sister Elizabeth was born in May 1794; another sister who died four months later was born in January 1796, another, Mary, in June 1797, another, Hellen, in September 1799, Margaret in January 1801, and John in January 1806. All his biographers agree that from an early age he displayed that eccentric behaviour which earned him the name of "mad Shelley." His relation to his mother is not revealed directly in any infantile reminiscence, but we do have his poem on a cat composed presumably when he was eight years old and certainly not later than when he was fourteen. The important stanzas are as follows:

You would not easily guess
All the modes of distress
Which torture the tenants of earth;
And the various evils,
Which like so many devils,
Attend the poor souls from their birth.

One wants society,
Another variety,
Others a tranquil life;
Some want food,
Others, as good,
Only want a wife.

But this poor little cat
Only wanted a rat,
To stuff out its own little maw
And it were as good
Some *people had such food,*
To make them hold their jaws!

This poem, I believe, may plausibly be taken as an unconscious irony against the devouring, orally castrating pre-oedipal mother. Shelley does not mention the gender of the cat but we are told that at the age of six he memorized Gray's *Ode on the Death of Favourite Cat* upon hearing it recited only once. Gray's poem is pretty clearly the basis for Shelley's and fills out its unconscious intent, for Selima loses her life while trying to catch two goldfish. This poem is, of course, not sufficient evidence to conclude that Shelley was then struggling with an unconscious conflict with the pre-oedipal mother image, but it is worth taking in connection with other evidence. It may also be noted in passing that as a youth he attempted one or two masochistically provoked plagiarisms.

But Shelley's story about Dr. Lind who sometime between his sixteenth and eighteenth year was called upon to reassure him that his father would not commit him to an insane asylum shows that he had succeeded in using the oedipus conflict as a defense against the oral conflict soon after he reached the age of puberty. This defensive shift of aggression from mother to father came to a climax in his expulsion from Oxford for atheism. The events leading up to this break show that he was unconsciously and masochistically provoking his father to reject him and, indeed, on a deeper level there was also a rejection by the mother image involved—for was not Oxford his alma mater? The association with T. J. Hogg is pretty plainly an unconscious homosexual one, but it is now no longer possible to tell to what extent this effiminacy in Shelley was traceable to genuine oral causes, and therefore true homosexuality, and to what extent it was due to the negative oedipus complex where the feminine identification would create a spurious homosexuality.[3] We may note, however, that there are a few indications that in the last few years of his life Shelley was beginning to be conscious of his effeminacy. Such is the transformation of himself as Prometheus into the feminine earth symbol. Such too is his choice of the name Ariel—drawn from Shakespeare's *The Tempest* where the fairy has a hermaphrodite character. If Shelley did become conscious of these effiminate traits we may be sure that he was suffering from spurious homosexuality only. On the other hand Shelley's paranoiac traits as attested by his delusions of persecution and the voyeuristic fantasy of seeing eyes in Mary Godwin's nipples and other hallucinations before his death point to true homosexuality. Probably the tendencies stemming from both levels of regression reinforced each other. But although Shelley refused to part from Hogg (the name has oral connotations!) at his father's command, he nevertheless could not satisfy himself with male friends for as long as Wordsworth, Coleridge, or even Keats. For no sooner had the enmity between Shelley and his father come into the open than he formed the connection with Harriet Westbrook, whom he plainly did not love, but whom he could easily take as an oedipal mother image since she too was plagued with a tyrannical father. As is typical in the negative oedipus relation, Shelley seems to have made a feminine identification with Harriet and thus fantasied that he was submitting to the tyranny of her father—an action which would serve as a defense against the aggression he was guilty of with respect to his own father.

This attempt to assert the oedipal defense soon deteriorated as a result of its negative oedipal form. Shelley was incapable of showing any real affection for Harriet and hence abandoned her to the attempted seduction of his friend Hogg. The masochistic tendency to submit to the father, characteristic of the negative oedipal relation, appears in the hallucinatory story of the murderers who attacked him at Keswick at about this time as well in his willingness to forego the large income to which he would fall heir if his father would pay him an annuity of 200 pounds. Significantly, he asked that the remainder of his due share should be divided between his mother and sisters. The defensive nature of this last request appears in the fact that about the same time he accuses his mother à la Hamlet, of adultery with a certain Edward Graham. There is a similar masochistic hallucination several years later at Tanyralt where Shelley not only claimed to have been fired at—probably an unconscious attempt to carry out the obsessive thoughts of suicide which plagued him—but also says that he saw a devil standing outside the window. He subsequently drew a picture of this devil and its one obvious feature is that the devil has horns. This may be an allusion to his father again since in accusing his mother of adultery he had said that Graham might be exonerated of "cornuting old Killjoy's brow," that is, being given cuckold's horns, largely because there was so little temptation!

The importance of Shelley's quarrel with his father in 1811 is seen in the fact that the first ideas for *Promethcus Unbound* appear in his letters to Eliza Hitchener at this time. Thus Shelley's expression of the negative oedipal relation in real life bore fruit years later in its expression in the poem. But it should be noted again that in Shelley's case the oedipal conflict is a defense against the earlier oral conflict. Unlike a true oedipal neurotic he was incapable of sustaining his affections for any one woman for long. Hence he had to reject a series of lady friends who included Harriet Grove, Harriet Westbrook, Eliza Hitchener, Cornelia Turner, Mary Godwin, Emilia Viviani, and Jane Williams among others. The pursuit of each new woman after the estrangement with the last was mainly an attempt to prove that he did not hate mother after all. It was also a way of playing one woman off against the other and putting them all in the wrong as far as Shelley himself was concerned. Unconsciously for him they were all untrue. His oral conflict is also apparent in his vegetarianism as well as his peculiar habit of unconsciously tearing off pellets of the bread he was eating and shooting them at the faces of people. The lavish magic gestures which he executed with his father's money are also typical of the oral type. Finally we may note his attraction to the water and sailing coupled with his inability to learn to swim. On several occasions he came near drowning on this account; once while sailing with Byron on Lake Geneva, once while bathing with Trelawny in the Arno—at which time he lay motionless at the bottom until Trelawny fished him out. Shelley then said: "I always find the bottom of the well, and they say that Truth lies there. In another moment I should have found it, and you would have found an empty shell." Shelley does not say that Byron had used the same proverb in *Don Juan* and personified Truth in feminine terms. It is symbolically significant that he should have lost his life by drowning.

VI

BYRON

Don Juan

THERE are several puzzling questions which occur to the reader of Byron's *Don Juan,* particularly when he comes to it with some knowledge of Byron's earlier poems. The earlier poems are for the most part serious to the point of being histrionic, but *Don Juan* is satiric if not downright cynical. What were the motives which drove Byron from these early expressions of the romantic agony to the now bitter, now good-humored badinage of *Don Juan?* Whatever these motives were, they did not only affect the tone of *Don Juan.* We can see them at work in the vicious attack which Byron directs unceasingly at Wordsworth, Coleridge, and Southey, the pioneers of the Romanticism in whose name Byron paradoxically attacks. It is true that these three had in Byron's opinion become despicable political reactionaries, but he could, in spite of this, have respected them for their literary achievements. For the presence of these polemics in a poem whose narrative theme is not primarily political must strike one as strange. This double rejection of the established prophets of Romanticism and the serious style which they had helped to introduce finds a paradoxical corroboration in the fact that the authority of Pope and the neo-classical style is invoked against that of Coleridge and Wordsworth, while at the same time the picaresque verse of *Don Juan* flouts every canon of neo-classical taste.

The answers which a psychological examination of the poem's structure will give to these questions will, I think, throw considerable light on the unconscious meaning of the poem. But before we consider the significance of the episodes of the story we may note that the second motto with which Byron heads the poem is the famous quip from Shakespeare's *Twelfth*

Night: "Dost thou think, because thou art virtuous, there shall be no more cakes and ale? Yes, by Saint Anne, and ginger shall be hot i' the mouth, too!" This jibe at a too rigid standard of Puritan morals uses the oral pleasure of "cakes and ale" as irrefutable touchstone of right living. May this not be the first hint that the key to Byron's complex psychological motivation, as for all the poets we have discussed thus far, lies on the oral level of regression? This suspicion is strengthened when we read the fragment which Byron wrote on the back of his MS of Canto I and which now stands at the beginning of the poem in the Oxford edition.

> *I would to heaven that I were so much clay,*
>   *As I am blood, bone, marrow, passion, feeling—*
> *Because at least the past were pass'd away—*
>   *And for the future—(but I write this reeling,*
> *Having got drunk exceedingly to-day,*
>   *So that I seem to stand upon the ceiling)*
> *I say—the future is a serious matter—*
>   *And so—for God's sake—hock and soda water!*

Here again, for what it is worth, is a hint that the poet's deepest problem in *Don Juan* is an oral problem. But as soon as we approach the Dedication of the poem, we are thrown off the track. We are at a loss to see the reasons for the abrupt attack on the "Lakers." Granting the conscious political motives, we still wonder why it is necessary to begin a poem about an amorous and picaresque hero with an attack on political reactionaries—or even political reactionaries who are bad poets. There is, however, a clue in the appeal to Milton in stanza x. For Milton is lauded as a "tyrant hater" who never yielded in spite of the worst misfortunes. He is thus an oedipal hero along the lines of Byron's Manfred, Mazeppa, and so on, whereas the "Lakers" in succumbing to the principle of tyranny are examples of the negative oedipal hero who because of his feminine identification must appear in a cowardly and unstable role. But there is also a hint that this oedipal allusion may after all be only a façade. For among Milton's chief persecutors appear his "heartless daughters," thus suggesting that he has not only to contend with the tyrannical father image, but also with an unresponsive pre-oedipal mother image. Perhaps this ambiguity in the sex of the enemy appears in the fact that Castelreagh is termed an "intellectual eunuch."

But our deduction as to the negative oedipal character of the Lakers gains added significance when we see that Byron begins the first canto by saying that his poem lacks a hero. He rejects the various martial heroes,

French and English—nine-farrow of that sow, the goddess of fame—which the age has to offer. Instead he chooses Don Juan who he implies is in some sense not a real hero. As we shall see, what Juan lacks is that very air of Byronic rebel which is typical of the positive oedipal hero. Juan, it will appear, is a negative oedipal hero, and this will in large part account for the effeminate behaviour which Byron frequently ascribes to him. Perhaps the most significant factor in Juan's effeminacy is suggested by Byron's telling us that Donna Inez, Juan's mother, has been the dominant force in his childhood. His father, Don José, died at the height of an unequal struggle to hold his own against Donna Inez. This means that Juan has only his mother to imitate and struggle against and his subsequent career, like Byron's own, will be largely determined by this fateful fact. The first attack against this mother is begun with the ridicule of her bluestocking pretensions—especially as they evidence themselves in Juan's education. Byron devotes a stanza to pointing out the homosexual aspect of Anacreon's, Sappho's and Virgil's poetry—the relevance of which to Juan's effeminacy is clear. Similarly Donna Inez does her best to protect Juan from other evil influences which his education might expose him to.

But it is all in vain, for Juan's first amatory adventure is hardly such as does credit to the pains his mother took for him. His first affair is as illicit as it well could be. Donna Julia, the young wife of fifty-year-old Don Alfonzo, is, however, far from being a pure and naive innocent falling into the hands of a ruthless seducer. On the contrary Byron does not suggest that it was Juan who took the initiative at all. It is Donna Julia who has the center of the stage and forces herself on Juan's attention. This once more underlines Juan's effeminacy, but it is not the most important point about this episode. For it is really an attempt to show Juan in the role of the positive oedipal hero who, instead of waging his major conflict with the mother image, attacks, though really by way of defense from the conflict with the mother, the father. Byron makes it clear that this is his intention by remarking that Don Alfonzo is reputed to have had an early affair with Donna Inez. The possibility thus exists that Juan may be his son and that Donna Julia stands in the place of the oedipal mother whereas Donna Inez holds that of the pre-oedipal mother. This distinction is perhaps emphasized by Byron's remarking that Donna Inez was not much concerned to hinder the progress of the love affair between Juan and Julia—rather strange for a real mother concerned for her son's moral welfare, but not strange if we consider that we are dealing with two different levels of infantile aggression.

But despite the sanction of the pre-oedipal mother to this new turn in the conflict which at least gives her a respite, we find that Juan's thoughts while courting Julia suggest that he is really preoccupied with the pre-oedipal mother. Byron compares his feelings to those of Ovid's Miss Medea —a classical prototype of the bad pre-oedipal mother—and says that he was "tormented with a wound he could not know" in order to stress the pre-oedipal masochistic elements. The upshot of his speculations as he wanders disconsolately in the wood is that he is late for dinner, a typical oral disappointment. We are further told that summer is a dangerous season for love due to the sun, and this is again suggestive of pre-oedipal aggression. And finally the actual declaration of love between Juan and Julia takes place under the chaste aegis of the moon as Juan rests his head upon Julia's bosom. Thus it is that Byron breaks into the love scene with an apostrophe to Plato as the sponsor of sublimated homosexual love as opposed to the more truly heterosexual love of the positive oedipus relation.

> Oh Plato! Plato! you have paved the way,
>   With your confounded fantasies, to more
> Immoral conduct by the fancied sway
>   Your system feigns o'er the controlless core
> Of human hearts, than all the long array
>   Of poets and romancers:—You're a bore
> A charlatan, a coxcomb—and have been,
>   At best, no better than a go-between.

Nevertheless Byron is determined to make a good showing with his oedipal façade and as we approach the bedroom scene we hear more of the sinfulness of pleasure in the context of Prometheus, Adam, and Waterloo —all of which symbolize the revolt of the son against the father principle! Moreover the night on which this scene takes place shows neither moon nor stars and thus suggests that the pre-oedipal mother is in abeyance. It is true that Byron burlesques the entire scene by saying that Don Alfonzo wants to prove himself a cuckold and by making Donna Julia ramble on at a great rate while the search for Juan is going on. She wonders at what quarter the moon is, in the midst of her torrent of recrimination, and has to call for a glass of water to keep up her voice. We can hardly take this defense seriously—especially since Juan is hiding all the while under the bedclothes, though Byron does remark that this sort of smothering is better than being drowned in a Malmsey butt of wine. However, the discovery of Juan's shoes by Don Alfonzo leads to a real oedipal fight between father and son. The forgotten shoes in themselves already forebode the castration theme. But the typical oedipal weapon, the sword, is soon knocked from Don Alfonzo's hand and only a disgraceful hand-to-hand struggle ensues. In the course of it Juan gets a bloody nose to indicate that it is he who deserves castration but finally is forced to flee like Joseph, another typically negative oedipal hero, leaving his clothing behind him. When he reaches the gate, he locks it from the outside, thus closing the door forever on the genital level of experience.

The episode ends with the announcement that Donna Inez has decided to send Juan on his travels and thus she reappears as the bad mother, the chief object of Juan's aggression. Julia on the other hand is dispatched to a nunnery whither Juan seems to have no desire to pursue her and which truly indicates her passivity as positive oedipal mother. She is no longer the benevolent giving mother, for her letter says that she cannot weep and that her "breast has been all weakness" on Juan's behalf. Byron ends the canto with an appeal to the prudish British public not to reject his shockingly immoral poem. For his homeland is for Byron one of the most fundamental of mother symbols by which he at once feels rejected and abandoned and which he must consequently attack in order to defend himself from his passivity. The entire poem is such an affront to the mother country before which Byron feels his basic passivity. There is also a defensive attack on Wordsworth, Coleridge, and Southey who as negative oedipal turncoats are again contrasted with the positive oedipal Milton, Dryden, and Pope. But all this display of defensive aggression only leads Byron to a passage which bewails in true masochistic fashion the vanity of life. At thirty he speaks as if he were an old man and decries even the fame, previously referred to as a sow, which his poetry will bring him.

All of this passivity is brought to a symbolic climax in the stanza which speaks of the futility of Cheops' pyramid. If we remember that the pyramids can be taken as breast symbols raised by a people masochistically preoccupied with death in a country where life depends on the great oral symbol of the flooding river, we can understand how important this passage is to the poem as a whole. But in order to retrieve matters a little before concluding the poem, Byron says that he is lucky things are no worse and advises himself to "read your Bible, sir, and mind your purse." The first half of this piece of advice reasserts the positive oedipal defense insofar as the Bible is the great textbook of patriarchal religion. The second half looks toward the negative oedipal defense insofar as it involves anal regression. On this latter point Byron will have more to say later.

Canto II opens with Juan's departure from his native country, an event which his unconscious interprets as a rejection by the pre-oedipal mother who withdraws her breast and leaves the poor infant to shift for himself. It is true that Byron throws up a preliminary defense against this coming attack on the pre-oedipal mother by paying some ironic compliments to the ladies of Cadiz. But we are soon told that Juan is being sent as a dove of promise, that is, like a hopeful bird-breast out onto the barren flood, by Donna Inez who in his absence significantly sets up a Sunday school for naughty children. Juan, for his part, is in an aggressive mood too for he refuses to read his mother's parting letter of advice. As he stands on board ship and watches the "growing waters" we are told that he feels "quite unmanned"—that is orally castrated. As his seasickness grows Byron recommends beefsteak as a remedy thus recalling one of the earliest forms of infantile aggression against the breast: biting with its association of raw meat. Moreover the thought of leaving the "most unpleasant people" makes one "keep looking at the steeple"—that is, the phallic breast. Juan weeps like the captive Jews who wept "by Babel's waters" and this allusion to the whore of Babylon is strengthened by a reference to Hamlet's disreputable mother as she strews flowers on the grave of the drowned Ophelia. His thoughts, like those of an abandoned infant, now turn to dying in exile as a result of his "thirst to see again thy shore" where Guadalquivir's waters glide. But the retchings which represent Juan's infantile rejection of the breast now grow worse. He calls for a glass of liquor but only becomes inarticulate—that is, incapable of giving words-milk. Byron tells us that he felt:

> The loss of love, the treachery of friends,
> Or death of those we dote on, when a part
> Of us dies with them . . .

The connection of all this with the pre-oedipal mother image is pointed up once more when we are told that Love cannot withstand colds and inflammations, bowel or stomach troubles, all infantile reactions to mother's lack of care, though it will "heroically breathe a vein," that is, thrive on aggression.

The storm which now overtakes the most holy Trinidada gains added meaning if we see it as an unconscious dramatization of the bad, denying mother whom the infant imagines as avenging its own aggressive rejection of her—symbolized in this instance by Juan's attack of seasickness upon his departure from his native country. It is thus significant that the ship first springs a leak so that the passengers have to man the pumps, just as the infant imagines that he will be drained by a mother who refuses to allow

him to keep what he has so strenuously drained from her. Of equal significance is the fact that the masts must be cut away to symbolize oral castration; and the fact that the sailors all attempt to get drunk but are kept at
bay by Juan with a loaded pistol to dramatize his identification with the
denying mother image. To strengthen this identification Juan is compared
to the ideal ascetic, Don Quixote, whereas his tutor, Don Pedrillo, who lies
speechless in his bunk, is compared to Sancho Panza. Provisions are now
got ready for those who are to abandon ship, for Byron says that "men,
even when dying, dislike inanition!" The daylight passes and the twilight
is like "a veil which if withdrawn would but disclose the frown of one whose
hate is masked"—perhaps the omnipresent mother image symbolized by the
sea over which the twilight lingers. There is also a remark to the effect that
those "who too much have quaffed" could alone see the grim humor in trying to embark on a raft in such seas. For the sea yawns and sucks down the
stricken ship leaving the hopeless survivors to drown or die of thirst and
hunger.

The sun rises red and fiery the next day to indicate that we have now
reached a high point in infantile aggression against the mother image. A few
teaspoonfuls of rum are served out to show how much mother denies, and
Byron, while digressing on the desire for life, mentions the castrating
shears of the most awful of the feminine Fates, Atropos. He also remarks
that men cannot, like woodcocks, live upon suction—though we might add
that the infant at the breast does—but, sharks and tigers, must have prey.
But after three days of calm in which "Ocean slumbers like an unweaned
child" the men become uncontrollable and fall ravenously upon their provisions and consume them all. They then turn to Juan's spaniel which we
are told was his father's dog to lend some color of oedipal defense from
Juan's point of view. They kill it and Juan, who feels "the vulture (bird-
breast) in his jaws," gets one of the forepaws but cannot eat it, for he is,
after all, a passive negative oedipal hero. The men are now reduced to eating caps and shoes as added castration symbols but their hunger, which is
compared to the Promethean vulture's, and Nature, which gnaws them to
this resolution, force them to resort to cannibalism. The oral symbolism of
this cannibalism is stressed by the fact that the physician, who dispatches
Pedrillo on whom the lot falls, chooses as his first portion the blood which
flows from Pedrillo's wrist—"being thirstiest at the moment." The oral
nature of the crime is further stressed by the fact that the men drink salt
water in order to wash down the flesh which in turn drives them mad and

makes them die despairing—a typical punishment for this most extreme form of aggression against the breast.

But these open hints at the oral crime must be screened on a higher level by an oedipal defense and accordingly Byron introduces an allusion to Dante's Ugolino who was forced to devour his own children and remarks that if foes may be food in hell (Ugolino gnaws upon his enemy's skull there) it is certainly permissible to dine upon one's friends at sea. This oedipal façade is strengthened by the fact that two fathers watch their sons expire in their arms. The result of this redirected aggression is that rain begins to fall as the preoedipal mother seems to relent. It is sucked into their parched mouths as it is absorbed by a piece of sailcloth—again the breast symbol. Furthermore a rainbow—the promise that mother will no longer send a flood—appears in the sky. It is called an airy child of vapour and likened to a bow that's bent and a crescent to symbolize the aggression at a distance of the pre-oedipal child-mother relation. Moreover a beautiful white bird, like the dove which brought the olive branch to Noah's ark, appears as a symbol of the reconciled breast. The long-sought-for land of mother earth comes in sight. Now mountains appear as symbols of the harmless breast, while two sharks follow the boat to symbolize the evil breasts from which Juan is escaping, though he does so by clinging to an oar—perhaps a symbol of submission to the negative oedipal penis.

Juan is now the sole survivor, for the other men, who were such things "a mother had not known her son" among them, have died of starvation and thirst. As Juan struggles through the surf to shore the dreadful sea mother nearly sucks him back into her insatiate grave, but he finally manages to fall down at the entrance of a cliff-worn cave which is to symbolize the womb from which he is to be reborn. He lies upon the sand like a withered lily whose mouth like a cup needs only to be filled with dew. Consequently when he revives, the first thing he sees is Haidee's small mouth bending over him and the first thing his own lips feel is the cordial which she pours between them. But as if to disclaim these hints that the newborn infant's first contact with reality is an oral one, he reverses the roles and says that Haidee watches "with eagerness each throb that draws a sigh from his heaved bosom." She now takes him into the cave whither the aggressive rays of the sun-son cannot penetrate and we are treated to a highly ambivalent description of Haidee herself. Her eyes, symbolic of the passively recipient mouth, are black as death, her glance is swift as an arrow, or a coiled snake which hurls its venom. But her lips are sweet even though she herself is a model for a statuary—shades of the Medusa! There is also a remark on an Irish lady's bust to which Byron never saw justice done!

But while Haidee and Zoe prepare food and fire for Juan, Byron reminds us that Haidee has a father who will certainly resent this intrusion of Juan's. Moreover the father has a connection with the sea-mother and conveying Juan to his house is like conveying to the cat-mother the mouse. But for the present Juan sleeps untroubled by the rushing of the neighboring rill or the young beams of the excluded sun. Haidee on the other hand has Juan's aggression projected upon her and dreams of a thousand wrecks and handsome corpses strewed upon the shore. Early in the morning she rises and with face flushed by blood which is compared to an Alpine torrent checked at the base of a mountain like the Red Sea she hastens to Juan. She finds him asleep like an infant, even though sleep, Byron tells us, is awful—perhaps because Haidee bends o'er him still as death and drinks his scarce drawn breath. She is the lady of the cave and he is her shipwrecked boy. Juan's passivity is further stressed when Haidee forbids Zoe to awaken him and give him breakfast—so a second breakfast must be prepared. In the meanwhile Juan lies with a purple hectic on his cheek, like dying day on the snow tops of distant hills-breasts, hushed as the babe upon its mother's breast. When he first opens his eyes, Haidee forbids him to close them again and Juan's thoughts, as in prayer, turn from grisly saints and martyrs hairy suggestive of masochistic orgies to the sweet portraits of the mother of Christ.

At this point Haidee again forbids Juan to talk and though he cannot understand her words they sound to him like the warble of a bird, the sort of sound we echo with a tear (masochistic attachment to the breast) though it also has an overpowering tone like melody that descends as from a throne. Significantly Juan's thoughts turn to breakfast and chiefly a beefsteak. This in turn leads Byron to introduce an allusion to the dreadful myth of Pasiphae to whom he gives the credit for making the Cretans the lovers of war and bulls. But feeling still the famished vulture Juan falls upon the breakfast prepared by Zoe like a priest or shark—perhaps allusions to the sharks which followed Juan to shore and the servant of the Virgin whom Juan adores. But though Haidee is said to watch him like a mother and be willing to feed him past all bounds, Zoe must remind her that famished people must be slowly nursed else they always burst. Consequently Juan is once more refused the nourishment he so ardently desires, though he is told that he has already gorged enough to make a horse ill. He is now clothed by the women and since he cannot understand Greek, he learns to understand the language of female lips and eyes.

Thus Juan's love for Haidee is born. She comes in every morning, rather early for Juan who was somewhat fond of rest, to see her bird reposing in his nest. We are told that returning health and idleness are as oil and gunpowder to passion's flame, thus hinting at the aggressive aspect of this love, and that Ceres and Bacchus are also great adjuvants to Venus, thus pointing to its oral character. This latter point is followed by an interesting stanza on amatory foods. The happiness of the lovers grows apace even though Haidee looks upon this her first love—and her last—like a rich wreck, an ocean treasure. A month passes, after which her father puts out to sea leaving her free as a married woman to enjoy Juan as she pleases. As the lovers saunter idyllically on the wild and breaker-beaten coast and watch the sun set opposite the moon, Byron digresses to tell us the oral pleasures of wine, and women. For significantly the best of life is but intoxication and after long travel, ennui, love, or slaughter nothing can vie with that draught of hock and soda water. In short Byron is saying that Juan's and Haidee's love has really regressed to the oral level and that all is well there. Thus the red sun of infantile aggression is setting and the mountain crescent and the broad rising moon symbolize the benign pre-oedipal mother. They cling to each other like swarming bees—but as if the image of the queen bee leading her colony to a new hive were too heterosexual in content, Byron adds that their hearts were as flowers from whence the honey sprung thus indicating that Juan and Haidee are like worker bees who alone gather honey and are of neuter sex. Most of the images which are now used to describe Haidee and Juan's love are drawn from the oral level of experience. Haidee flies to her young mate like a young bird, their intense souls poured into each other as her heart beats passionately against his bosom. Byron stresses their helpless baby state by remarking that it is a pity that such lonely innocence must be paid for with hell fire and the Stygian river. Nevertheless the moon sheds benignant light upon them as Haidee's breast warms to Juan's pale cheek. A remarkable series of comparisons again point to the oral and anal levels on which this love is consummated.

> *An infant when it gazes on a light,*
> *A child the moment when it drains the breast,*
> *A devotee when soars the Host in sight,*

> *An Arab with a stranger for a guest,*
> *A sailor when the prize has struck in fight,*
> *A miser filling his most hoarded chest,*
> *Feel rapture; but not such true joy are reaping*
> *As they who watch o'er what they love while sleeping.*

Byron also speaks of the unconscious joy with which Haidee's heart is over-flowing and which nevertheless has some strange resemblance to death without terrors. The ambivalent note is sounded again when we hear that the love of women is a fearful thing and that their revenge is as the tiger's spring. On the other hand we are told that man, to man so oft unjust, is always so to women.

From here to the end of the canto Byron oscillates between the poles of this ambivalent conception of love on the oral level. Haidee is spoken of as Nature's bride—we remember that Nature is a feminine personification —and as passion's child. Further clues which repudiate heterosexuality are that Juan and Haidee's priest was solitude and that each was an angel—hermaphrodite. Yet the masochistic tinge of such pregenital love is not forgotten. Byron exclaims: "How much it costs us!" and says that Love is the very god of evil whose inconstancy makes all men cuckolds. It also makes men philosophers in the gloomy sense of that word and in a cynical passage Byron tries playfully to justify inconstancy as nothing more than admiration of nature's rich profusion. But over the changing skies of the heart there always lingers some vague darkness and destruction, and the liver which is the lazaret of bile produces not only first love but also rage, fear, hate, jealousy, revenge, compunction, which are said to be like knots of vipers on a dunghill's soil.

These paradoxical comments on a love so pure as Haidee's and Juan's are continued at the beginning of Canto III. Haidee is now said to be deeply blest to feel the poison through her spirit creeping, or know that Juan resting on her bosom was a foe to rest. There is an apostrophe to Love, in which we learn that it is fatal to be loved and love's best interpreter is a sigh. Those who dote on flowers place them upon their breasts but to die. There are more cynical remarks to the effect that after her first love woman treats love like an easy glove, that love and marriage rarely can combine. Even men get a little tired of love since the same things cannot always be admired. Worse still we are told that all tragedies end with death and all comedies with marriage and hence we may argue that death and the lady have a good deal in common. Hence too only Dante and Milton could write of Heaven and hell—or marriage which is the same thing—because they were unlucky in love. It is true that Haidee and Juan are not married but the indulgence of their innocent desires is still illicit.

All of these hints of Juan's unconscious aggression against the pre-oedipal mother image now force Byron to erect once more the oedipal defense and so we begin to hear of Haidee's returning papa. There is first some cynical justification of his ruthless and rapacious character on the ground that his piracy is nothing but what a prime minister calls taxation. More important, however, is the fact that Byron speaks of him as Ulysses, a returning husband or a sire and thus he can in some sense be thought of as Haidee's husband and Juan's father. Significantly when he lands he finds a great feast in progress to symbolize the oral nature of Juan's and Haidee's love. The father symbol is being placated by some children who are wreathing a white ram. Still as an unweaned lamb, the patriarch of the flock all gently cowers. Worse still the father is burlesqued by an impotence symbol in a dwarf buffoon who is telling stories of magic ladies such as Circe who transform men to beasts. And Byron adds that pleasure (whene'er she sings at least) is a siren. Finally we learn that the reason for all this merrymaking is that a rumor of Lambro's death has brought Juan and Haidee into their inheritance and at this there is general rejoicing. Such a mistake in itself is enough to infuriate the father and to make matters worse all of the servants he encounters are so drunk that they cannot answer his questions coherently.

Byron has thus presented Lambro as the avenging oedipal father and even suggested that his return as from the dead is in the capacity of husband. But Byron also stresses the fact that he is not in high temper as we might expect the positive oedipal father to be. On the contrary he has manners bland and though he lies coiled like a boa in the wood, he is still the mildest-mannered man. This may perhaps be partly accounted for as an ironical understatement of Lambro's really violent character. But it may also be accounted for by the fact that Byron traces his piratical profession to a reaction against the slavery which was his lot as a Greek. Thus his despair to save her, his country, had stung him from a slave to an enslaver, and he waged war in vengeance of her degradation. Here we see that the ambivalent character of Lambro's personality is related to the mother image as personified in his native country. His identification with his enslaved mother country makes him a negative oedipal son and hence effeminate like Juan. But we soon hear that the loss of his daughter's affection was sufficient to wean him from all milk of human kindness and turn him mad with blindness like the Cyclops. He then becomes like a cubless tigress or the ocean in storm and Byron descants on the vanity of putting your hope in children—though it is true that it is beautiful to see a matron bring her children up (if nursing them don't thin her)! All these allusions and comparisons point to Lambro's connection with the mother image.

Byron now sketches in the oral background against which the oedipal defense is to be raised. He describes the dinner which is going forward in Juan and Haidee's apartments with all its voluptuous pleasures. Nevertheless we are reminded at the same time that there is no sterner moralist than pleasure. The infantile basis for this inhibitory caution is hinted at in the sun emboss'd in gold on the scarlet cushions and the description of Haidee herself in which we note such details as that beneath her chemise her breast heaved like a billow, or that her white baracan flowed round her like fleecy clouds about the moon, or that her auburn hair flow'd like an Alpine torrent which the sun dyes with his morning light, or that her eyes like glossy rebels mocked the jetty stain, and in their native beauty stood avenged, or finally that the gems beneath her baracan were like stars on the milky way. There is perhaps further evidence that the real enemy in the coming conflict is the mother image if we consider some of the details Byron gives us about the poet who could or would have sung to these lovers. Although there was a time when his fortunes were o'ercast due to his seeming independent in his lays, he has now become a turncoat like Wordsworth, Coleridge, and Southey and sings the sultan and the pacha, or what is the same, "God save the king." But although he is a sad trimmer the presence of Juan, who is about to submit to the negative oedipal relation, forces him to sing a hymn which in its positive oedipal purport, at least, serves as a warning and defense for Juan.

But though the song is a call to rebellion against the tyrannical-father principle, there is much in it which shows the poet's infantile passivity and aggression before the pre-oedipal mother image. Thus the first glory of Greece which comes to mind is not Homer or Archilochus but the reputedly homosexual poetess, Sappho. She serves as an excellent symbol of pre-oedipal aggression because her very femininity disguises the fact that she rejects the feminine sex due to her violent pre-oedipal aggression. Perhaps for this reason the poet ends the stanza by saying that all the glories of the Greek islands have vanished except their sun—the symbol of pregenital aggression. The poet next turns to the oedipal defense in the stanzas which describe how the Greeks repulsed the tyrant Xerxes at Marathon and Salamis. But he is uncertain whether such redirected aggression is possible in his own day. He speaks of the lyre having degenerated into his hands and thinks of turning his hymn into a drinking song by way of oral regression. This leads to an allusion to another great and reputedly homosexual Greek poet—Anacreon. His maleness, however, comes dangerously close to revealing the true object of the poet's aggression. Consequently we are told that Anacreon served a "good" tyrant in the Nemesis-pursued Polycrates. Here we have the cue for the negative oedipal defense, for this lover of freedom and hater of all tyranny now cries: "O, that the present hour would lend another despot of the kind!" The poem now continues in the drinking-song vein and the poet sheds tears to think that the virgins dancing in the shade—to think such breasts must suckle slaves. His last stanza places him on Sunium's marbled steep where he prays "swan like, let me sing and die." We thus end on a direct and symbolic allusion to the power of the breast complex.

The purpose of the song, as well as the preliminary description of Lambro, has thus been fulfilled. It was primarily to express the poet's aggression against the pre-oedipal mother image. But this approaching repression of his aggression forces Byron to a display of cynicism which is outstanding for its repudiation of the art to which he owes the poem. For poetry is itself a form of aggression against the mother image. The poet gives himself words-milk in autarchic fantasy and thus excludes the need for the mother's doing so. But since aggression is to be forbidden, the very fame which the poet has justly earned must be decried. He will be remembered only because his name will turn up in the refuse found in digging the foundation of a closet. Milton, though famed for being an independent, was nevertheless humiliated by being whipped at college—that is, by his alma mater. There is a satirical allusion to Archdeacon Coxe's part in preserving the great Marlborough's fame. Southey comes in for a sneer and Wordsworth's *Excursion* is ridiculed. His *Waggoners,* indeed, serves as the occasion for advising him to pray Medea for a single dragon.

Having taken care of these matters Byron can now proceed to end the canto with the calm and beautiful stanza appealing to the benevolent mother image of the Virgin Mary. The dwarfs and the dancing girls are temporarily banished and the benediction of the Ave Maria sinks o'er the earth so beautiful and soft. He prays that our spirits may dare look up to hers and her son's, though Mary's own eyes are downcast beneath the Almighty dove. The poet tells that his devotion is to Nature whose altars are significantly the mountains and the ocean, earth, air and stars—and all that springs from the great Whole. The sweet hour of twilight weaves its spell, though there are ominous allusions to the spectre huntsman of Onesti's

line and his hell dogs—perhaps a distant allusion to the huntress goddess
Diana. Then comes the famous translation of Sappho's lyric to Hesperus,
the evening star—with Byron's significantly altered line:

> *Thou bring'st the child, too, to the mother's breast.*

But it is also the hour when sweet friends are torn apart, which fills with
love the pilgrim on his way, and which moves Byron to cry: "Ah, surely
nothing dies, but something mourns." Even the tyrant Nero, in premonition
of the negative oedipal submission to come, merits a pathetic tear and some
hands unseen have strewed flowers on his tomb. But the last two stanzas
jerk us from sentiment back to burlesque. Nero is now a sovereign buffoon
who has no more to do with the hero than the man in the moon!

As the fourth canto opens Byron tells us that he feels it difficult to
make a beginning. Plainly the change from positive to negative oedipus is
not easily made. It is like Lucifer's being hurled from heaven and then first
coming to know his weakness. But as the torrent of our hot blood widens towards the ocean we ponder deeply on each past emotion. So Byron's sere
fancy has fallen into the yellow leaf. So too he now laughs because he cannot weep. There is a bitter allusion to Achilles whose mother dipped him in
Styx though a mortal mother would have fixed on Lethe. But as Byron approaches his story he tells us that Pulci was sire of the half-serious rhyme in
which he sang of true knights, chaste dames, huge giant kings despotic—
all symbols of the positive oedipal relation. But this topic is obsolete and
hence Byron has chosen a more modern subject—the negative oedipal relation. There is also an allusion to the forthcoming castration in a mention
of Father Time whose rude scythe has cleft such gentle bosoms as those of
Juan and Haidee. Byron now speaks of their separation in typically oral
similes:

> . . . . *the tree*
> *Cut from its forest root of years—the river*
> *Damm'd from its fountain—the child from the knee*
> *And breast maternal wean'd at once forever,—*

And the theme of masochistic submission to both mother and father image
is finely summed up in the lines, "life's strange principle will often lie deepest in those who long the most to die." The oral basis for the coming action
is further stressed when we hear that Juan and Haidee were like children
born from out a rill to pass their lives in fountains, and Byron adds that
there was no more reason for their loves than for those of nightingales and
doves.

Together the lovers watch the sinking sun. A faint low sigh escapes from Juan's breast and Haidee's long black prophetic eye lets fall a tear at the thought of their having to part. Byron makes a jaunty remark about their denying augury with a kiss to the effect that both women and wine are maladies one must undergo. But Juan and Haidee gaze on each other with looks which mingle the feelings of friend, child, lover, brother and which makes them beings passionate as Sappho's song. And as they slumber in their loneliness, which Byron compares to that of songbirds brooding on the nest, Juan's frame feels an occasional shudder while Haidee's lips murmur like a brook or deep clear stream within an Alpine hollow. Significantly it is she, as Juan's feminine identification, who dreams that she is chained to a rock, like Andromeda, against whom the sea-mother rages. Next she is pursuing something white and indistinct, perhaps the breast again, with bleeding feet, and finally she is in a cave where her tears turn to stone and fall on Juan dead and cold at her feet. It is clear that she and not her approaching father is her lover's worst enemy.

Byron's intuitive understanding of the various regressive layers involved can be seen in the action which now takes place. Haidee's first impulse is to throw herself in front of Juan's body which is suddenly menaced by Lambro's pistol. In this way Juan's own reaction to the father image is symbolized. For although Juan seizes a sabre, he cannot and will not be permitted to play the role of the positive oedipal son. He is to be the negative oedipal son and his feminine identification with the mother image is symbolized by Haidee's action. On the other hand Byron points to the defensive nature of both oedipal relations by remarking at this point that Haidee and her father are alike even to the delicacy of their hand. Thus we may guess that Juan's conflict is not merely with the father image, but with the mother image as well since Lambro bears Haidee's likeness. This latter likeness is accentuated when Juan and Haidee are parted and Lambro's arms coil around her like a serpent, while his men rush on Juan "as darts an angry wasp." Juan receives a token castration by being wounded on the arm and head from which the blood flows like a little brook and then is transported to the seashore—that is, to mother!—where he is chained on board a galley. Byron here takes leave of him, though moved by tears—which he says are like a Chinese nymph than whom Cassandra, who foretold another oedipal tragedy, was not more prophetic. Further oral associations are brought forward in an appeal to that Naiad of the Phlegethontic rill, Cogniac, who like other nymphs makes her lovers ill.

Juan's case, however, is not so bad as Haidee's whose bosom bounds with worse pain. Byron tells us a little of her youth in the land where the olive rains its amber store, where grain gushes from the earth, and poison trees and long deserts, and roaring lions betoken her character as pre-oedipal mother. Her very eyes show passion's force sleeping like a lion near a source. Up to this moment she had kept her soft and milky way, incapable of terror to the earth and tempest to the sky; but the sight of Juan cut down and like a cedar felled unlooses all the pre-oedipal aggression which has hitherto been hidden. Significantly she turns it against herself and like a lily lies o'ercharged with rain at the brink of death. For days she lies with vacant eyes, though they attempt to wean her from her frenzy with music. At this she becomes violent against all near her. In typical oral regression she refuses food and soon death takes her and Byron remarks that soon or late Love is his own Avenger.

We now return to Juan whose slave ship is nearing the scene of old Troy where thoughts of the ancient glory of Achilles and Patroclus are brought to mind—not unappropriately in view of Juan's approaching feminine role. But the plain of Troy which was once a battlefield is now only a pasture for quiet sheep. There are further hints of Juan's effeminacy in the fact that he falls in with a company of Italian opera singers who are also being sold into slavery. They have the reputation of being castrati, or as Byron says, members of the third sex, and to make it doubly clear there happens to be an odd male and an odd female so Juan is chained with a soprano who has masculine traits. Nor is Juan moved by the lady's charms. Byron remarks that it may be because no one "can hold a fire by thought of frosty Caucasus." For the moment even the author's aggressive impulses seem to be in abeyance and he says "I'm fond of yielding" and "I wish to part in peace" as regards his critics and detractors. Anyway Fame is valueless as a snowball and sinks beneath its offspring's doom. The young De Foix is commemorated by a broken pillar and Dante by a little cupola. Byron himself abdicates his fame which is wholly in the power of those "benign ceruleans," the patrician "left-legs" known as the blue-stockings. It is in this mood of total submission to the mother image that Juan is put up for sale in the slave market at Constantinople.

The fifth canto opens with further allusions to various symbols of oral submissions. Venus' doves, St. Sophia's cupola, Petrarch as Plato's pimp, the charming Mary Montagu, the dangerous breakers of the Euxine, the Parcae, and the shivering slaves who stand as eels to be flayed, all contribute to the forthcoming humiliation of our hero. In the slave market Juan meets another victim of that fickle lady, Fortune, a victim who advises against rebellion which is as if "the corn sheaf should oppose the sickle."

Johnson has had three wives, the first died, the second ran away from him, and he ran away from the third. But in spite of this bad luck he is optimistic and tells Juan that there are still many rainbows in the sky. Love is only the first net spread for him. The other passions are the glittering lime twigs of our latter days. A eunuch now begins bidding on this superior yoke of human cattle who like typical oral regressives feel their loneliness and helplessness in terms of hunger. Byron adds that Alexander thought the act of eating, with another act or two, makes us feel our mortality in fact redoubled. But this look at the oral basis of Juan's predicament is immediately countered with an allusion to the military commandant, perhaps an oedipal father figure, whom Byron saw slain "the other evening" with five slugs. By the time we are through this digression, Juan and Johnson have been purchased and taken to the palace of the Sultan.

At this point Juan suggests to Johnson that they make an attempt to escape, but Johnson says his hunger must be satisfied first. He cannot withstand that all-softening, overpowering knell, tocsin of the soul—the dinner bell. They are led into a large empty room in which a marble fountain echoes. It is now that Juan's feminine transformation must take place and Byron appropriately says that nothing saddens him more than an enormous room without a soul. For a room is a feminine symbol and there solitude has her full growth and melancholy haunts long galleries. This leads Byron to mention the tower of Babel, a convenient breast symbol, which he says was Nimrod's hunting box in a city where the king of men, Nebuchadnezzar, took to grazing and Daniel tamed the lions. Here too lived the Queen who conceived an improper friendship for her horse. All of these images from the oral level of regression are prelude to Baba the eunuch's command that Juan dress himself as a woman, that is, complete his feminine identification, and submit to circumcision, castration. Juan finally submits to the former but not to the latter, though Johnson says he will make no objection and consequently he is led off to supper whereas Juan is taken to the apartments of the Sultana. Byron describes the gigantic portal through which he must pass and which is adorned significantly with battling warriors and guarded by ugly little impish dwarfs. These impotence symbols who usher Juan into his feminine world are mutes whose serpent optics seem poisonous to indicate their oral relations.

The Sultana Gulbeyaz before whom Juan is taken is a type of the imperious-mother image to whom it is our hero's fate to be always masochistically attached. She is described as Venus rising from the wave with a beauty of an overpowering kind that would strike the reader blind could Byron do justice to it. She is compared to Mary Queen of Scots, the unlucky mother of the unlucky Stuarts, and later to Diana, the goddess who strikes men with lunacy. Her features are said to have all the sweetness of a devil and her despotic and tyrannical character are emphasized by the poniard she wears at her girdle. It is not surprising that Juan should only be capable of bursting into tears when commanded to love this awe-inspiring creature, but we can now see that it is a fear motivated by his dread of the pre-oedipal phallic mother image which Gulbeyaz's poniard suggests. Furthermore his oedipal defense is now in its negative feminine phase and hence he cannot love her in any masculine sense. The masochistic aspects of the relation are pointed up by telling us that Gulbeyaz' words were like Arab spears and her tears like a pike—to Juan. But in spite of her threats and entreaties Juan only replies "the prison'd eagle will not pair." She is now appropriately spoken of as a tigress or lioness robbed of her cubs and Byron devotes a stanza to the strength of mothers' love for their babes and sucklings—for this is really the true relation between Gulbeyaz and Juan. Her wrath is like a short glimpse of hell, or like the ocean warring against a rocky isle and she wishes only to "kill, kill, kill." Her first thought is to cut off Juan's head and her next to stab herself. But Juan's own aggression is stronger and she feels humiliation flow in as water through an unexpected leak. Fortunately for Juan the whole scene is brought to an end by the unexpected appearance of the Sultan to do the offices of a real husband. And though Juan escapes the mother, it is at the expense of being mistaken for a real woman by the Sultan. This is the nadir of passivity.

The next three cantos have a prose preface which contains a strong attack on the Marquis of Londonderry—an attempt at positive oedipal defense, perhaps, since that is no longer possible in poetry. There is also an attack on public opinion, as another projection of the Super-Ego, for its censure of the morals of the poem. The canto itself opens with a remark about the tide in the affairs of women which, taken at the flood, leads—God knows where. Nevertheless Juan seems to be censured when Byron commends Antony, and incidentally himself, for having lost the world for love—or perhaps Gulbeyaz is the world which he loses for his love of Haidee. It is true that this love is now impossible for him and it is true that Gulbeyaz is cruel from inanition or lack of love, but Byron still offers the amorous tribe that cold comfort of Horace: *Medio tu tutissimus ibis*. Realizing that this motto is hardly appropriate for a typically dashing Juan he apologizes by saying that no one virtue yet, except starvation, could stop that worst of vices—propagation. Having arrived at this impasse Byron is ready to curse everything and everybody—except womankind, who, of course, are too dangerous for this stoical-masochistic philosophy. No, Byron loves the sex, and sometimes would reverse the tyrant's wish that mankind only had one neck to pierce. He once wished, not *now*, that womankind had but one rosy mouth.

But back to Lilliput, the land of the impotents. Juan is escorted into the sleeping quarters of the harem, admiring the backs and the breasts of the ladies as he goes. To stress his effeminacy Byron tells us of the sentimental friendship, extremely pure, which springs up between Juan, Lolah, Katinka, and Dudu. The gentle Dudu, who is compared to a soft landscape of mild earth, is chosen as Juan's bedfellow and she shows him through the harem and uses so few words that she is said to be silent thunder! The passivity of these two prompts Byron to recall the time when he himself played the lady's maid, though he adds that he loves wisdom—the lady— more than she loves him. We now have a description of various sleeping ladies. One smiles through her dreams like the moon, another has a pallid aspect, another is a frozen rill or snow minaret on an Alpine steep, another is "certainly aged." It is plain we are mounting to a climax and at this point Dudu screams and awakens the harem—all except Juan who lies as fast as ever husband by his mate. The ladies crowd around like waves of ocean, bosoms, arms, and ankles glancing bare, while Dudu describes the dream which frightened her. It is a dream of a golden apple-breast which she cannot reach but which finally falls down of its own accord after she has thrown stones at it. But just as she is about to eat it, a bee flies out and stings her lip. There could be no better key to the sort of love possible between oral regressives, but the matron ascribes it all to the fullness of the moon. Moreover, the dream is prophetic of Juan's approaching conflict with the Sultana. The Sultan has left her to take care of some urgent business with Catherine of Russia—greatest of all sovereigns and whores. Gulbeyaz now hears of what went on in the harem during the night. Her rage knows no bounds. Her brow is pale as a lily's. She stands like a pythoness, her tresses like those of a weeping willow. She orders the execution of Juan and Dudu.

Canto the seventh opens with an apostrophe to Love and Glory, libido and aggression, and since Juan has not fared very well with either of these, it is not surprising that we should have an unusually high quantity of cynical remarks at the beginning of this canto. Thus he says:

> *. . . I hope it is no crime*
> *To laugh at all things—for I wish to know*
> *What, after all, are all things—but a show?*

Various authorities are named to lend credence to the statement that life is not worth a potato. We live and die, but which is best, he says, you know no more than I. All of these cynical attacks on the Super-Ego are, of course, defenses against the hero's passivity. And since Juan has now reached the nadir of passivity, we may expect some violent defensive aggression. This duly appears in the account of the siege of Ismail at which Juan and Johnson arrive after their escape from the harem. Byron tells us nothing of this latter event—aggression is a better defense than mere escape. We shall see later why the escape must be hushed up. But no aggression could be more violent than that to which we are now treated. Byron first calls upon the aggressive goddesses of the *Iliad* to inspire him. There is a cacophonous passage of Russian names similar to Homer's catalogue of the ships. Fame is called a strumpet. Potemkin is said to have been made great through harlotry and homicide. Suwarrow himself is compared to a gas lamp presaging a most luminous attack—this via the identification words-knowledge-milk. Or he is like a will-o'-the-whisp along the marsh so damp. It is he who inspires his men with a thirst for glory gaping o'er a sea of slaughter. He drills his men just as you'd break a sucking salamander to swallow flame. So he appears now Mars, now Momus, a Harlequin in uniform.

It is at this point that Juan and Johnson appear before him. He accepts them into the armies of the Christian Empress and promises to run a plough over Ismail's proudest mosque whose domes are proper breast symbols. The ladies who have escaped with Juan and Johnson are given all attention possible and the men prepare to burn a town that never did them harm. Byron once more calls upon Homer to aid him in his warlike song, though he realizes it is as vain as for a brook to cope with ocean's flood. But the canto ends with a remark that war does little more than raise "sucking heroes" who turn out in the end to be nothing more than butchers in great business. Medals, rank, ribbands, etc. are as purple to the Babylonian harlot and if you want to know what Glory is—ask the pig that sees the wind.

Canto VIII gives us the battle proper. The army issues forth like a lion from his den or like a Hydra from its fen. The Danube's waters shine like a mirrored Hell and the ramparts blaze like Etna when the Titan hiccups in his den. The oral connotations of these images are plain and Byron takes

care to repudiate them by saying that the drying up of a single human tear
has more of honest fame than shedding seas of gore—that is, by another
oral image. Over against this, Wordsworth is quoted and censured for making Carnage God's daughter in his *Thanksgiving Ode*. But the cannon continue to throw up their emetic and thirty thousand muskets fling their pills
like hail to make a bloody diuretic. Why do men plunge so easily into this
red Vesuvius? Because like a pad, a hawk, or bride they are broken in to
fight like fiends for pay or politics. They are like travelers who follow over
bog and brake an *ignis fatuus* and they climb the ramparts as cheerful as
children climb the breasts of mothers. It is true that none of them willingly
go through destruction's jaws into the devil's den, and they would fain be
rid of the idle apprehensions roused by battle—apprehensions which like
wind trouble heroic stomachs. For after all the men are falling as thick as
grass before the scythes, or corn before the sickles.

Nevertheless Juan walks amidst such scenes as if he had been nursed
there. The thirst of glory pierces through him in spite of his feminine feature, in spite of the fact that from a child he had felt like a babe upon a
woman's breast. But Juan hates cruelty and before we are treated to his
aggressive climax, Byron defends his hero and himself from the reproach of
wantonly attacking the mother image—now looming through the mist of
battle in the form of the crescent, symbol of the mother-moon goddess, surmounting the city of Ismail—by giving us a digression on Daniel Boone!
Boone was a true child of Mother Nature, an active hermit who never
brought a frown on his Mother's unwrinkled brow. Crime came not near
him—she is not the child of solitude. So much for Nature—but here in
civilization the babe and mother upbraid Heaven with distant shrieks. Here
Lt. Col. Yesouskoi kills all the Turks he meets but cannot eat them. Here
death is drunk with gore. Here the heat of carnage, like the Nile's sodden
slime, engenders monstrous shapes. Here a dying Turk fixes his teeth on the
Achilles tendon of a trampling Russian and though decapitated he still
holds his bite. If the Pharisaic times, with all their pretty milk-and-water
ways, are shocked, Byron replies, "I sketch your world exactly as it goes."

But Juan and Byron need a still better defense than Boone against the
aggressive attack on the mother which they are perpetrating. Juan must reverse the roles. It is not true that he makes the mother terrible and cruel:
she is a little harmless child. It is not true that Juan wishes to attack her:
he rescues her from two dreadful Cossacks, avenging breasts. It is thus, in
the midst of battle, that we are introduced to the little female child with
palpitating breasts, Leila. The same blow which killed her mother has

scarred her brow, but Juan holds up a crucial attack so that she can be safely bestowed behind the lines. Having thus placated the mother image momentarily, Juan must also do the same for the father image—for one of his current defenses is that of the negative or passive oedipus relation. This is accomplished by the episode of the heroic Turkish father whom Juan and Johnson repeatedly beg to surrender because he is such a good, plain, old temperate man. But he is unmoved by their friendly overtures and strikes at his friends as babies beat their nurses. So they have no choice but to pour blows upon him like rain upon a sandy plain that drinks and still is dry. Four of his sons are killed and the fifth dies heroically as he is granted a vision of those black-eyed houris that make the Moslem fight. This is too much for the old man and he flings his breast against Russian steel as carelessly as the moth her wing against the light.

Byron and Juan are thus surrounded with both oedipal and pre-oedipal defenses and can now be as violent as they please against the pre-oedipal mother. Consequently the attack goes forward with renewed horror. The old pacha still holds out among the smoking ruins. He is said to be calmly smoking his hookah like a babe at the breast! But his valor is of little account now, for the crescent's silver bow has sunk and the moonlight on the water is imaged back in blood, a sea of slaughter. There is a brief digression on Wellington in order to point out that Ireland's famine feeds fat upon his glory and that due to his victories gaunt famine never shall approach the throne—though Ireland starve! This allusion to the connection between war and famine again strengthens the oral basis of the aggression and Byron excludes its genital source by pointing out that the Russians ravished very little—except for the six old damsels each of seventy years who were all deflowered by different grenadiers! But the source of aggression is the breast complex. Ismail flashes her burning towers o'er Danube's stream and redly runs his blushing waters down. And Byron manages to find among the ranks of the aggressors themselves a mother symbol who becomes an easy target for some of his most vicious satire. It is Catherine herself. When Suwarrow writes his victory dispatch: "Glory to God and to the Empress, Ismail is ours," Byron exclaims in italics *(Eternal Powers! such names mingled!)* He says he will teach the stones to rise against earth's tyrants and future ages will then find war as much of an enigma as we now find the pyramids—again the breast symbol. Nevertheless Byron concludes the canto by saying that he has drawn less with the long bow than his predecessors and his last words are reserved for the homeless, houseless, helpless orphan with whom he has provided Juan.

In Canto IX Byron and Juan are still concerned to defend themselves from the highly aggressive attack on the mother image represented by the siege of Ismail. This new defense is accomplished by projecting the guilt for unwarranted aggression on the Duke of Wellington who is accordingly attacked with great vigor and bitterness. He is denounced for having repaired legitimacy's crutch and supped full on flattery. Not only has he undone mankind in war, but his own country's and Ireland's starvation are due to him. At all this death laughs, and Byron cries, "Mark, how its lipless mouth grins without breath." This leads to further cynical remarks on the vanity of life. Men are as bubbles on an ocean much less ample than the eternal deluge which devours suns as rays, worlds like atoms. The only real problem in life is the problem of suicide: to be or not to be, as Hamlet said. Fame is useless, even if one is Alexander or Hephaestion, Alexander's homosexual lover. A good stomach will easily overbalance such abstract fame for there is an inward fate which makes all Styx through one small river flow. And yet life is not just a mere affair of breath. Byron sometimes thinks that life is death. In any case there's no such thing as certainty and perhaps doubt itself may not be doubting. The climax and purpose of all these cynical remarks come when Byron asks why his public has called him a misanthrope. The answer comes in italics: Because *they hate me, not I them!*

We can now return to Juan who is on his way to Moscow to carry Suwarrow's victory dispatch to the Empress. Though Juan is presently to become Catherine's lover, Byron denounces her at the climax of several stanzas which give vent to his detestation of tyrants and sycophants. The latter are human insects, catering for spiders. Catherine, who typifies the former, is to be gratified with a dispatch where blood is talked of as we would of water and where carcasses are said to lie thick as thatch o'er silenced cities. But Juan is secure in his rescue of little Leila who is a better trophy than the monuments of Nadir Shah, that costive sophy—the first hint that Leila is really Juan's anal birth fantasy. He appears before the Empress like Love turned a lieutenant of artillery and because she sometimes liked a boy and had just buried the fair-faced Lanskoi he is accepted in that "high official situation," a phrase which Byron explains with a sidestroke at that Sphinx, that long spout of blood and water, Castlereagh. Catherine, and women in general, are now apostrophized as, among other things, the gate of life and death, the perennial fountain in which all souls are dipped, the worst cause of war, the sea of life's dry land, and a desert which drinks Juan's news like summer's rain, and finally a whirlpool full of depth and danger.

Oh thou 'teterrima causa' of all 'belli'—
    Thou gate of life and death—thou nondescript!
Whence is our exit and our entrance, well I
    May pause in pondering how all souls are dipt
In thy perennial fountains how man fell I
    Know not, since knowledge saw her branches stript
Of her first fruit; but how he falls and rises
    Since, thou hast settled beyond all surmises.

Moreover the love between Juan and this lady is said to be like a quintessential laudanum or black drop whose first draught intoxicates the empress space—for the eye drinks all life's fountains (save tears) dry. Juan, for his part, is not fastidious because at his age all female ages are equal and so he is as bold as Daniel in the lion's den. And to make sure that we shall see Juan as wholly submissive to her, he is compared to a sun assuaging itself in the salt sea, while she is linked with Mary Queen of Scots, the goddess Pallas, Messalina, Clytemnestra, and Queen Elizabeth who is reprimanded for her stinginess—again an anal hint.

In the tenth Canto we are given Juan's rejection by the Empress and his dismissal to England—Byron's mother country which had rejected him and which he heartily disliked. That Juan is rejected by the Empress is not directly stated, but it appears from the fact that he cannot sustain his role as professional lover. Instead he becomes sick—the doctors say it is the harsh climate—and as a result must flee the country in ignominious defeat. Byron might easily have found other more heroic reasons to get his hero on his way. Instead he chooses to give us several ingenious defenses to counterbalance Juan's masochistic submission to the Empress-mother image. The first of these is a reassertion of the seriousness of his poetic mission which he has several times previously disparaged. We are told that man fell with apples in Adam's case and rose with them in Newton's case. The triumphs of modern science Byron accordingly hopes to equal in poetry and thus fares undauntedly out upon the ocean of eternity in his still seaworthy skiff. This is as much as to say that the aggressive self-sufficiency which the writer expresses when he gives himself words-milk is not being abdicated. There is another and slightly different defense in the stanzas in which Byron takes time out to forgive his mother country Scotland for some quarrels with her.

But by the end of the canto Juan has already arrived at the outskirts of London which appear to him like a half-quenched volcano, a huge dun cupola, like a foolscap crown on a fool's head. Byron concludes with a reprimand for Mrs. Fry for having preached to the poor rogues instead of the real people at fault. But he cuts himself short and says, "by and by I'll prattle like Roland's horn at Ronscevalles' battle." Thus he promises another full-scale attack on the mother image which is represented now by his native country. At the beginning of canto eleven, however, we find him worried by a problem in tactics. The weapons with which England is to be attacked are satire and ridicule. But these imply doubt, and doubt is not very conducive to creative activity. Thus he must appeal to doubt to "spoil not my draught of spirit, Heaven's brandy." Doubt indeed is a sort of indigestion which continually works confusion of the sexes. There seems to be only one remedy for this self-damaging ailment and that is more self-damage. Byron says that he has lately grown rather pthisical and as a result "as I suffer from the shocks of illness, I grow much more orthodox." There is moreover another way in which the attack on the native country can be justified. Suppose she attacks him first? This can be very easily arranged as we see in the brief episode where Juan is held up by robbers on Shooter's Hill. But Juan protects both his money and his life by killing the robber, called the moon's late minion, who would take from him the two things which alone have value to him now.

Juan continues his way into the metropolis under the pallid light of the moon. The Thames is apostrophized and the streetwalkers are duly noted. The diplomats are described as preparing to pounce upon Juan (who we learn has not been given a title by Catherine) like woodland hawks upon a songbird. Still diplomats are only liars and this is one thing Byron admires in women—that they can't do otherwise than lie! But socially Juan makes a great hit. He is received with much *empressement*—Byron has to borrow a term from French because it seems that the sea (see Billingsgate) has made the tongue more free in islands than on the continent. Juan is specifically approved of by the Blues, that tender tribe, who now come in for considerable ribbing at Byron's hands—the mother image attacked as learned lady. And so the canto continues with innumerable little pinpricks of satire and wit directed at British society and all leading to the question: "A moral country?" and the blunt reply: "You are *not* a moral people."

In the twelfth canto we find Byron catching up and at last motivating several events in the preceding cantos which seemed disconnected before. We remember that Juan's defeat by Haidee's father and his transformation in the Sultana's harem had signified his flight into the negative oedipus relation. Now one of the typical reactions to the negative oedipus relation is an unconscious regression from the oedipal level to the anal level.[1] On this level the child reverses the passive experience of being penetrated as he defecates—an experience which is associated with the passive penetration of the mouth by the breast—and produces an aggressive fantasy wherein the oedipal father's penis penetrates him. Thus his feminine identification brings him to demote the mother, whose role he is playing, to a child. This child, whether as a consequence of the coitus fantasy or as an independent symbol of the identification, is Juan's little Leila. Byron does not express these fantasies directly in the poem but there are several hints to show that they are at work. The first is the amorous glance which the Sultan casts upon Juan when he spies him among the Sultana's ladies in the harem. On the following night there is apparently a coitus scene between Juan and Dudu though Byron does not make it clear whether Juan plays the masculine or feminine role. More important still is the fact that from this time to his appearance at the siege of Ismail we know nothing of Juan's adventures. Perhaps silence was the best way of passing over the embarrassing pregnancy! And finally there is Juan's discovery of Leila just at the moment when his defensive aggression is at its highest point. Thus his aggression is not merely a defense against the feminine identification of the negative oedipus relation in general, but also against its nadir of passivity which has produced the anal birth fantasy which brings little Leila to him.

Canto twelve further substantiates these suppositions, for in this canto the English gynocracy is to deprive Juan of his charge and thus afford Byron one more proof that his native country is a denying castrating mother image to him. But even so there must be some compensation for this loss, and Byron finds it in singing the praises of the love of money as opposed to the love of women. This is quite typical of anal regression and simply means that if his first anal birth, Leila, is taken away, he can find another in his gold. Byron thus begins the canto by saying that he has reached the barbarous middle ages of life—he was about thirty-five at this time—an age which is a bore and which convinces us that love or lust makes man sick and wine much sicker. At this time of life the pleasure of money is the best bower anchor. The frugal life has ever been praised by saint and cynic. The mere hope of gold allures nations athwart the deep, but the miser possesses the ore. For him the Indies yield their fragrant produce and the cars of Ceres groan upon the roads, and the vine blushes like Aurora's lip. In the end he has the pleasure of leaving behind some dome surmounted by his meager face. So Cash rules Love the ruler on his own high ground, as virgin Cynthia sways the tides. Love is indeed prohibited except that which can be called matrimony and matrimony in turn is dependent on a man's ability to calculate his means of feeding brats the moment his wife weans.

With these remarks to compensate for the loss of Leila, Byron tells us that Juan is forced to relinquish her by sixteen dowagers, ten unwed she-sages and others whose follies had run dry and who pursued novelties like butterflies as food for inanition. This formidable phalanx makes Juan choose a certain Lady Pinchbeck as Leila's stepmother and without more ado Byron drops this episode and turns to another which he tells us is to form the beginning of the poem. We are surprised to hear that all that has gone before, twelve of the sixteen cantos he completed, is only a prelude to the poem proper. Yet as an expression of Juan's regressive tendencies it is easily understandable why Byron should say that these cantos are only an introduction to the first episode of Juan's mature life. This episode was to concern the problem of providing Juan with a wife, but though he approached the matter through four cantos he never lived to complete the story and see his hero married. For this reason it will perhaps be best not to include these unfinished last cantos in our analysis.

It only remains to answer briefly the question proposed at the beginning of this chapter: Why did Byron shift to satire and cynicism in *Don Juan* when so many of his early poems had been in a more serious histrionic style? The early poems had been for the most part strong expressions of the positive oedipal defense—the surest defense against an oral conflict. But as Byron grew older the oral conflict became more acute and the oedipal defense broke down. As a result, and as we have seen in our analysis of *Don Juan*, he was forced to retreat to less characteristic defenses: negative oedipal and anal. These more passive defenses forced him to grasp at every straw which he could use to demonstrate his aggressive defense. Satire and cynicism were thus confused attempts to turn the tables on his tyrannical inner conscience which was accusing him more and more of passivity. By means of satire and cynicism he projected the Super-Ego onto society and then proceeded to attack it there with laughter and sneers. The result was the brilliant patina of wit which glitters on the surface of *Don Juan*.

As a child Byron could not complain of his mother's neglect because she was busy with other children. He was an only child, but with such a mother this was a greater catastrophe than if she had totally neglected him. From the earliest years of his life he seems to have reacted aggressively to her fits of temper. The incident of the saucer which he seems to have attempted to devour in one of these early tantrums indicates the length to which he could go. And as if the conflicts with the mother were not enough there was in overplus his disreputable nurse, Mary Gray, who seems to have made life miserable for the boy. But we should not forget that this early aggressive behavior toward the two women closest to him was probably only defensive.[2] For Byron's real difficulty seems not to have been aggression but passivity. The extent to which his personality was capable of absorbing masochistic pleasure is seen in an anecdote from the year 1798 when Byron was ten years old. His mother had put him under the care of one Lavender who was to correct his lameness. In the words of his biographer Mrs. Colburn Mayne.[3]

The method adopted for the 'cure' was to rub the foot with oil, then forcibly twist it round and screw it up in a wooden machine. . . . Byron's teacher at this time was one Dummer Rogers, who read Latin with him; and Rogers one day broke out in urgent sympathy . . . "Such pain as I *know* you must be suffering, my Lord!" "Never mind, Mr. Rogers," said the boy. "You shall not see any signs of it in me!"

It should be remembered here that Byron always blamed his mother for his lameness. Further anecdotes which show his eagerness to put himself in situations where he would suffer physical or psychic pain can be found scattered all through his biography. He even wanted to *appear* unhappy as is seen from the following amusing anecdote related by his sculptor Thorwaldsen.

He placed himself opposite, but at once began to put on a quite different expression from that usual to him. "Will you not sit still?" I said to him; "you need not assume that look." "That is my expression," said Byron. "Indeed?" said I, and I then represented him as I wished. When the bust was finished, it was universally admitted to be an excellent likeness. Byron, when he saw it, said "It is not at all like me; my expression is more unhappy."

He intensely desired to be so exceedingly unhappy; added Thorwaldsen with a humorous expression when he told this story to Anderson.

In addition to Byron's strong masochistic tendencies there are also numerous oral traits which show that his passivity related to the pre-oedipal phase of infantile development. Among these we may note the famous "thinning campaign" by means of which Byron tried to avoid the corpulence which was a legacy from his mother. He seems first to have begun dieting when he was at Cambridge though it is not recorded whether he got the idea that he could not bear to see a woman eat at the same time! (The latter idiosyncracy was strictly enforced by him so that he either dined alone or in male company. It is plain here that Byron was satisfying an unconscious masochistic wish to be starved. He shifted the blame, however, by saying, "No, it is not I who wish to starve myself, on the contrary I force mother to starve herself.") It is worth noting that the year following his ostracism from England Byron intermitted the "thinning campaign" for a time while residing at Venice. He immediately grew very corpulent—as much as to say, "While mother England idolized me, I had to starve to prove her in the wrong. Now that she has really rejected me, I can grow fat again." In the last years of his life, however, when his good name was returning, the thinning campaign was resumed. Byron's unconscious wish to starve mother extended to parsimony wherever women were concerned. Mrs. Colburn Mayne states that there are scarcely more than two instances of his generosity toward women. One was toward a certain Mrs. Mule, his charwoman, "of whose gaunt and witchlike appearance," says Moore, "it would be impossible to convey any idea but by a pencil;" and the other was to a woman in Ravenna to whom he granted a weekly pension for the rest of her life. She was, however, ninety-five years old at the time! We may also note the American artist, Benjamin West's, acute observation of the connection between Byron's masochistic and oral traits.

I remember once telling him, that notwithstanding his vivacity, I thought myself correct in at least one estimate which I had made of him, for I still conceived that he was not a happy man. He inquired earnestly what reason I had for thinking so; and I asked him if he had never observed in little children after a paroxysm of grief, that they had at intervals a convulsive or tremulous manner of drawing in a long breath. Wherever I had observed this, in persons of whatever age, I had always found that it came from sorrow.

In the opinion of Lady Blessington, one of Byron's shrewdest observers, his mouth was the most remarkable feature in his face. All of these observations, of course, point to Byron's relation to his mother. Indeed, he seems even to have transferred his grudge against her and his nurse to the university of Cambridge. About a year after his M.A. was granted in 1808 he wrote to a friend: "*Alma Mater* was to me *injusta noverca;* and the old beldam only gave me my M.A. degree because she could not avoid it."

There is a good deal of evidence that Byron numbered unconscious homosexuality among the aggressive defenses against his masochistic attachment to the mother image. At Harrow where he displayed a very pugnacious and rebellious external behavior he nevertheless made several tender friendships with his fellow students, chief among which was that with Lord

Clare whom Byron said "he always loved better than any *(male)* thing in the world." This remark was made just before his death in one of the last letters from Missolonghi. New male friendships were formed at Cambridge but a young chorister named Edelston seems to have been one of his deepest attachments. In his Ravenna Diary of 1821 he said of this relationship that "a violent, though *pure,* love and passion— which held me at that period— were the then romance of the most romantic period of my life." We may mention one other such attachment: Nicolo Girard, a young Frenchman, whom Byron met on his first Continental tour in Greece. His affection for this young man went so far as to make him a legatee to the extent of 7000 pounds in his will of 1811; but then, Byron was always very generous in money matters to all of his male friends. It may be worth noting at this point that in the same will of 1811, Byron stipulated that he should be buried with his dog—perhaps again a homosexual fantasy defense.

There is, however, also evidence that Byron's homosexuality, like Shelley's, was of the spurious sort which is really a feminine identification on the negative oedipal level. His effeminacy in behavior was not so conspicuous as Shelley's but nevertheless remarked upon by several contemporaries—notably Lady Blessington who found his voice effeminate. Others were surprised to find that the satanic hero put his hair up in curl papers! More positive proof, however, is to be found in the fact that Byron seems to have been quite consciously attracted to masculine women who satisfied his need for feminine identification. While at Cambridge he kept a mistress in London whom he would dress up in male attire and pass off as his brother Gordon "in order that my mother might not hear of my having such a female companion." The celebrated affair with Lady Caroline Lamb is partially explained by the fact that Lady Caroline was an aggressive and unpredictable woman who liked to dress up in page's costume and visit Byron in this fashion. It is clear, indeed, that Byron played a passive and unmasculine role in most of his love affairs. He said that the beauty of Lady Adelaide Forbes, another of his amours, was the very image of the Apollo Belvedere. On his wedding night he asked if his wife intended to sleep with him and said: "I hate sleeping with any woman but you may if you choose." The fact that all of these homosexual hints were quite conscious shows that Byron's homosexuality was a spurious and not a more deeply repressed unconscious defense.

The evidence for Byron's negative oedipal complex which he uses as a defense in *Don Juan* centers around his relations with Mary Chaworth and his wife Isabella Milbanke. His love for Mary seems quite clearly to have been an oedipal defense against his pre-oedipal conflict with the mother. It was a safe defense against his pre-oedipal conflict because he knew that Mary was engaged to another man and would have none of him. At the same time it was a plausible means of shifting his unconscious aggression from the mother image to the father image. Mary was a relative of his and thus his love for her could easily stand for mother love. On the other hand Mary's grand-uncle had been murdered by Byron's uncle (the one from whom he inherited his title) in a duel and thus Byron could easily think that in wooing Mary he was poaching upon enemy territory—that is, territory of the father. This supposition is borne out by the fact that Byron had a superstitious dread of the ancestral portraits in Mary's house. He thought they had "a grudge against him because of the Duel, and to be ready to come out of their frames and haunt him." This aggression against and dread of the father is typical of the negative oedipal relation, but its defensive character as an escape from a conflict with the mother image is apparent in Byron's remark when he learned of Mary's marriage: *"This* threw me out again 'alone on a wide, wide sea.' " The sea, as in *Don Juan,* is one of Byron's symbols for the mother image.

In 1811 Byron's mother died just after he returned from his first Continental tour. There had been a severe blow to his aristocratic pride when he had been refused precedence by the British ambassador at Constantinople—a fact which may account for Don Juan's feminine humiliation there. In this same year several close male friends also died. All these events pointed to the weakness of Byron's defenses against his basic conflict. He may have reproached himself unconsciously for the death of his mother and the loss of male friends may also have been taken as punishment for his aggression against the mother. In desperation Byron seems to have determined upon the strongest oedipal defense possible to him—an incestuous relation with his half-sister Augusta. A child of this union was born early in 1813. But Byron evidently could not maintain this positive oedipal role for long. His love for Augusta *was* a successful switch of aggression from mother to father, but he could not be satisfied until he also achieved the masochistic passivity which is characteristic of both the pre-oedipal and the negative oedipal conflict. This he accomplished by negotiating the respectable marriage with Isabella Milbanke in 1814. He admittedly had no love for her and all his friends advised against his marriage with this rather bluestocking young woman who was associated in his mind with his mother by the fact that on the same day that he received her long letter of acceptance (of which he flippantly notes in his *Journal,* "It never rains, but it pours!") his gardener also found his mother's long-lost wedding ring. As a consequence, unconsciously of course, he managed to torment his wife in various ways until the law, which personified father to him, forced a separation and society, representing his mother, ostracized him from England. Thus he finally achieved in real life the negative oedipal defense which is expressed in literary form in *Don Juan*. Another instance of the negative oedipal defense may be seen in Byron's dealings with the Prince Regent. He was first highly flattered by an introduction to the Prince. Later he wrote a satirical poem which was calculated to humiliate the Regent. When he heard of the latter's reaction he said: "I feel a little compunctious as to the Regent's *regret:*—would he had been only angry! but I fear him not."

It is thus remarkable that in both Byron's and Shelley's case, the only long poems which they wrote which are still universally praised are based upon the negative oedipus defense which we have seen was specific for them in real life too. *Childe Harold* in Byron's case may be claimed as an exception, but this is scarcely a unified poem in the sense that *Don Juan* is. It is also interesting to note that Byron refused to accept payment for *Childe Harold* as for most of his early poems. This suggests that he unconsciously looked upon literary composition as forbidden aggression and thus thought payment for it to be conscience money. He was willing, however, to accept payment for *Don Juan,* but at this time he was becoming more and more avaricious in preparation for the final masochistic denouement in Greece. This avarice appears in *Don Juan,* as we have already noted, in the Leila episode. The aggressive character of *Don Juan* is seen in one of Byron's remarks to Murray concerning revisions in the poem: "I am like the tiger; if I miss my first spring, I go grumbling back to my jungle."

NOTES

Chapter I   1) A survey of relevant quotations from artists is given in mund Bergler's essay in *Psychoanalysis and the Social Sciences*, edited by Geza Roheim, 1947. This paper also contains a survey of psychoanalytic theories on literary production as well as a brief statement of Dr. Bergler's own contributions to the topic. See also his forthcoming *Writers and Psychoanalysis*.

2) See for example Chapter II of Frederick G. Hoffman's *Freudianism and the Literary Mind*, 1945; "Psychoanalysis and Literature" in *The Columbia Encyclopedia of Literature*, 1947.

3) Of Freud's later works, *The Ego and the Id, Beyond the Pleasure Principle*, and *Civilization and Its Discontents* are most important in this connection.

4) See Edmund Bergler, *The Basic Neurosis*, 1949.

5) The identification of words-milk, or in its most general significance as the infant probably distinguishes it, sound-liquid, finds expression in phrases describing the poetic process in almost every poet in the European tradition. Such, for example, are the common idioms "a flood of words," "fluent speech," "a flow of language," and so forth. In poetry more elaborate images frequently depend upon the mythological fact that the Greeks made the Muses goddesses of poetry and the arts who lived on mountains such as Helicon or Parnassus and guarded sacred springs such as Castalia, Aganippe or Pieria. It was the liquid from these springs which inspired the poets and thus the myth admirably supports the theory that poetry stems from an oral level of the unconscious. The Muses may be taken as pregenital mother symbols, the mountains as breast symbols, and the springs as milk which issues from the breast. The prescribed offering to the Muses was milk and honey. Moreover, it should not be supposed that because this myth is very old, later poets used it unmeaningfully. Great poets are always quick to discard hackneyed images which are of no real value. The tenacity with which poets have clung to the myth of the Muses shows that it probably has deep psychological roots.

I shall cite here a few examples from the Romantic poets alone which employ the unconscious identification sounds-liquid. In some cases music is used metaphorically for poetry but basically words or thoughts are understood. In Coleridge's case perhaps the most remarkable instance of the identification is his characterization of himself as poet at the end of the fragment of Kubla Khan:

> . . . *Beware! Beware!*
> *His flashing eyes, his floating hair!*
> *Weave a circle round him thrice*
> *And close your eyes with holy dread,*
> *For he on honey-dew hath fed,*
> *And drunk the milk of paradise.*

The dome itself, of course, is a breast symbol. We may also note that in his theory of the romantic imagination he consistently terms it a fusing, diffusing, and dissolving power. The Latin roots of all these words point to the fact that imagination liquifies words. As a poetic example he cites a passage from Sir John Davies' *Nosce Te Ipsum* in which the process by which the soul *digests* ideas is being described. Similarly Wordsworth says that poetry is the spontaneous *overflow* of powerful feelings and speaks of imagination in the *Prelude:*

> The awful Power rose from the mind's abyss . . .
> . . . like the mighty flood of Nile
> Poured from his fount of Abysinnian clouds
> To fertilize the whole Egyptian plain.   V, 591 ff.

From Byron we have passages like:

> . . . thought, which—as a whelp
> Clings to its teat—sticks to me through the abyss
> Of this odd labyrinth; or as a kelp
> Holds by the rock; or as a lover's kiss
> Drains its first draught of lips;   DJ X, xxviii

And Keats in *Endymion* speaks of:

> All lovely tales that we have heard or read:
> An endless fountain of immortal drink,
> Pouring unto us from the heaven's brink.   I

For further examples see my article in *American Imago*, 1949. Shelley's "I pant for music," and *To the Skylark,* contain other instances.

6) Proof of Sophocles' homosexuality is given in Hans Kelsen, "Platonic Love," *American Imago*, 1942.

7) For a list of writers known to be homosexuals see Henri Peyre, *Writers and their Critics*, p. 179. It could be enlarged with other names such as Augustine, Marlowe, Bacon, Gray, Novalis.

8) In analytic literature Freud was the first to hint at the bird-breast symbol in his analysis of a dream of the orally regressed Leonardo da Vinci. Leonardo dreams that a falcon stoops from its flight and dips its tail into his mouth—an action which Freud interprets as a fellatio wish. There are also many cultural associations between bird and breast. In classical mythology love and mother goddesses such as Ishtar (a deity of war *and* fertility), Aphrodite (frequently associated with Ares), and Diana (huntress and guardian of childbirth) are often portrayed with prominent breasts symbolized by cones, and have their totem in the form of a bird—usually a dove. The Greek Muses were also winged and their connections with the breast symbol have already been noted. James Joyce's *Portrait of the Artist as a Young Man* contains a startling identification of bird and breast. The Egyptian god Thoth, the inventor of the art of letters, was ibis-headed and his Greek counterpart, Hermes, was winged. Both Egyptians and Greeks portrayed the flight of the soul from the body at death as a

bird, thus perhaps symbolizing the feeling of abandonment and desolation which the child feels when he is abandoned by the breast. In the Old Testament it is a dove, otherwise known as The Holy Spirit (*rūach*, feminine gender in Hebrew) and the instrument by which Holy Scripture was inspired and written, which moves over the face of the waters before the creation, and a dove which brings back the sign of the retreating waters of the flood. In the New Testament it is a dove which descends upon Christ as he ascends out of the waters of Jordan where he has undergone symbolic rebirth—as it also comes to the apostles when they speak with tongues at Pentecost. Perhaps the most ancient cultural association is to be seen in the prehistoric Lascawen cave paintings (ca. 20,000 *B.C.*). Here a bird-headed man in prostrate position is about to be gored by a bison (whether bull or cow is not clear) and beside him stands a bird totem stick. If the bird-breast identification is valid, we have a perfect icon of the masochistic results of the breast complex. A clinical example of this symbolism is given in Dr. Henry Bunker's "A Note on Ambivalence," *Psychoanalytic Quarterly* 1948.

Chapter II   1) Roy P. Basler, *Sex Symbolism and Literature,* 1947. Mr. Basler's essays contain some good general statements on the necessity for psychological interpretation of literature, but his contention that *Christabel* is a study of Lesbianism does not seem plausible to me. There is no evidence that Coleridge consciously intended this to be the case. From an unconscious point of view a homosexual defense could not be disguised in feminine identifications. If Coleridge had been unconsciously preoccupied with a homosexual defense in this poem he would, I think, have stressed Christabel's (and consequently his own) attachment to her father more strongly.

2) Other psychoanalysts have given more detailed accounts of the extent to which masochism permeates the personality. See for example: Edmund Bergler, *The Battle of the Conscience,* 1947, J. C. Flugel, *Man, Morals and Society,* 1945, and Karl Menninger, *Man Against Himself,* 1938.

3) See *The White Goddess,* 1947. This book contains a wealth of mythological and anthropological evidence corroborating the psychoanalytic theories which are advanced in the present book. Mr. Graves, however, makes no use of psychological theory to support his conclusion that poetry is written on one theme: "the question of what survives of the beloved."

4) This edition also contains an interesting footnote to the MS lines omitted from this passage in the published edition. J. A. Symonds in his life of Shelley comments on the line "Hidden, deformed and pale of hue," that it "is necessary to make common sense of the first and second part. It is the keystone that makes up the arch. For that reason Mr. Coleridge left it out."

Now this is a greater psychological curiosity than even the fragment of 'Kubla Khan' . . . Towards midnight on the 18th of July 1816 Byron recited the lines in 'Christabel' about the lady's breast; when Shelley started up, shrieked and fled from the room. He had seen a vision of a woman with eyes instead of nipples!" Shelley's voyeuristic fantasy stresses the importance of the breast complex as a key to the poem's unconscious meaning.

5) Ruskin is an interesting case of a writer who seems to have been dominated by this fantasy. See Edmund Bergler, "John Ruskin's Marital Secret and J. E. Millais's Painting 'The Order of Release,' " *American Imago*, 1948.

6) It is not known just how much Wordsworth related of the passage from Shelvocke's *Travels* which gives the incident of the shooting of the albatross, but one passage is of especial interest. Shelvocke says: "we had not the sight of one fish of any kind, since we were come southward of the streights of *Le Mair*, nor one sea bird, except a disconsolate black albatross" . . the one which the mate Hatley shot. The phrase "streights of *Le Mair*" contains a pun on the French word *la mere*. If Coleridge heard this detail from Wordsworth's lips there would have been added reason for his accepting the story of the albatross so quickly. We have already seen the possibility of such a pun in Coleridge's footnote to *Christabel*.

7) See J. C. Flugel, *Men and their Motives*, 1934, pp. 44 ff.

Chapter III   1) See Edmund Bergler, *The Basic Neurosis*, 1949.

2) Mr. Cleanth Brooks in his interpretation of this poem in his book *The Well Wrought Urn* has suggested that Wordsworth meant to correlate the "visionary gleam" of the *Ode* with his theory of the romantic Imagination. If we remember that unconsciously imagination is an exquisite sublimation of voyeurism as a wish to get and that this in turn is a defense against the wish to be refused, we have an unconscious basis for the statement.

3) Professor Lionel Trilling in the *English Institute Annual 1941* associates the visionary gleam with the pristine state of childish megalomania when there is no clear distinction between outer and inner reality. He very perceptively cites a passage from Book II of the *Prelude* where Wordsworth describes the child at the breast gaining its sense of reality under the presiding influence of the mother. The sense of pre-existence, of which Wordsworth speaks, is possibly reminiscent of that prenatal paradise within the womb from which the child is an exile. Professor Trilling cites both Freud and Ferenczi in discussing these points.

Chapter IV   1) The edition of Keats' *Poems* by Ernest de Selincourt cites *Hamlet*, i, 4, 8-12 and *Macbeth*, i, 7, 67 as parallel passages here and it is noteworthy that both these plays contain famous oedipal situations.

2) Keats originally wrote for lines 8-9, stanza xxxix:
> *Put on warm clothing, sweet, and fearless be;*
> *Over the Dartmoor black I have a home for thee.*

Professor de Selincourt remarks that this suggests that Madeline's future home "opened on the foam of perilous seas." If the association is valid, we would have another reason for thinking that Madeline and Porphyro have not really escaped the pre-oedipal mother.

3) For lines 174-76 Keats originally wrote:

> She fled into that valley they must pass
> Who go from Corinth out to Cencreas,
> The rugged paps of little Perea's rills.

The last line is a striking image involving the identification breast-stream.

4) The edition of Mr. de Selincourt cites Burton's *Anatomy of Melancholy* (pt. iii, sect. ii, mem. iii, subs. i). "So will she by him—drink to him with her eyes, nay drink him up, devour him, swallow him."

5) In a passage which Keats omitted at this point he describes Lamia's rage at Lycius' proposal of marriage. The passage following the quarrel is as follows:

> Which lov'd most,
> Which had the weakest, strongest, heart so lost,
> So ruin'd, wreck'd, destroy'd: for certes they
> Scarcely could tell . . . they could not guess
> Whether 'twas misery or happiness.
> Spells are but made to break.

Chapter V 1) It is interesting that in the notes to *Queen Mab* Shelley gave the following account of Prometheus' original crime: "Prometheus (who represents the human race) effected some great change in the condition of his nature, and applied fire to culinary purposes; thus inventing an expedient for screening from his disgust the horrors of the shambles. From this moment his vitals were devoured by the vulture of disease." He then goes on to quote from Newton's *Defence of Vegetable Regimen* which at this time was the authority for Shelley's own orally determined vegetarianism. "Thirst, the necessary concomitant of a flesh diet, (perhaps of all diet vitiated by culinary preparation) ensued; water was resorted to, and man forfeited the inestimable gift of health which he had received from heaven."

2) On this point see Carlos Baker, *Shelley's Major Poetry*, 1948, note to page 116 and Appendix III, 1.

3) See Edward Carpenter and George Barnefeld, *The Psychology of the Poet Shelley*, 1925.

Chapter VI 1) See Edmund Bergler, *The Basic Neurosis*, 1949.

2) Mario Praz in his *Romantic Agony* makes Byron into a sadistic prototype of the Satanic hero without taking into account the underlying passivity for which this show of aggression was the defense. He does cite with approval, however, Charles Du Bos who thinks that Byron's hyperactivity may have been due to *"un coeur en soi statique."*

3) Ethel Colburn Mayne, *Byron*, 1924, p. 24.